Studies in Funerary Archaeology vol. 16

"AND SO THE TOMB REMAINED"

Exploring Archaeology and Forensic Science Within Connecticut's Historical Family Mausolea

by
Nick Bellantoni

OXBOW | books
Oxford & Philadelphia

Published in the United Kingdom in 2021 by
OXBOW BOOKS
The Old Music Hall, 106–108 Cowley Road, Oxford OX4 1JE

and in the United States by
OXBOW BOOKS
1950 Lawrence Road, Havertown, PA 19083

© Oxbow Books and the author 2021

Paperback Edition: ISBN 978-1-78925-502-7
Digital Edition: ISBN 978-1-78925-503-4 (ePub)

A CIP record for this book is available from the British Library

Library of Congress Control Number: 2020947373

All rights reserved. No part of this book may be reproduced or transmitted in any form or by any means, electronic or mechanical including photocopying, recording or by any information storage and retrieval system, without permission from the publisher in writing.

Printed in the United Kingdom by Short Run Press

Typeset at Versatile PreMedia Service (P) Ltd

For a complete list of Oxbow titles, please contact:

UNITED KINGDOM	UNITED STATES OF AMERICA
Oxbow Books	Oxbow Books
Telephone (01865) 241249	Telephone (610) 853-9131, Fax (610) 853-9146
Email: oxbow@oxbowbooks.com	Email: queries@casemateacademic.com
www.oxbowbooks.com	www.casemateacademic.com/oxbow

Oxbow Books is part of the Casemate Group

Front cover: The Edwin Morgan Tomb, Cedar Hill Cemetery, Hartford, Connecticut (Photo: Nick Bellantoni).
Back cover: Pitkin Family Tomb, Center Cemetery, East Hartford, Connecticut (Photo: Brian Meyer).

To the memories of

David G. Cooke
John J. Spaulding

and

my father Frank

Contents

List of Illustrations vii
Acknowledgements xi
Map xiii

Part I. Tomb Restorations

1. Introduction: Moseley Tomb 3

2. Squire Elisha Pitkin Family Tomb 18

3. The Tomb of Gershom Bulkeley and His Descendants 33

4. The Tomb of His Excellency Samuel Huntington, Esq. 54

Part II. Tomb Vandalisms

5. Henry Chauncey Family Tomb 75

6. Edwin Denison Morgan Tomb 90

Glossary 111
Bibliography 118
Index 124

List of Illustrations

Map 1. Map of the State of Connecticut showing locations of the six family tombs explored in this book
Fig. 1.1. Restored Moseley and Gates/Troop Family Tombs, First Church Cemetery, East Haddam, CT
Fig. 1.2. Earliest dated burial marker in Connecticut, 1644, Rev. Huit, Palisado Cemetery, Windsor, CT
Fig. 1.3. Classic 18th-century iconographic New England headstone
Fig. 1.4. Cedar Hill Cemetery, "Rural" Cemetery Movement, marble burial monument of Samuel Colt in center, Hartford, CT
Fig. 1.5. The family tombstone of actress Katherine Hepburn, Cedar Hill Cemetery, Hartford, CT
Fig. 1.6. Pitkin Tomb Signage with Quick Response (QR) Code Bar, Center Cemetery, East Hartford, CT
Fig. 2.1. Pitkin Family Tomb, Center Cemetery, East Hartford, CT
Fig. 2.2. A 19th-century advertisement for the Fisk Metallic Burial Case
Fig. 2.3. Fisk Metallic Coffin of Dr Edward Pitkin and the Pulp-Fisk Coffin of his wife Carlissa Pitkin
Fig. 2.4. Squire Elisha Pitkin
Fig. 2.5. House of Squire Elisha Pitkin as it stood in East Hartford, CT
Fig. 2.6. French General Comte de Rochambeau
Fig. 2.7. Interior of Pitkin Tomb, showing coffins balanced on brick partitions
Fig. 2.8. Schematic showing positions of the coffins, interior, Pitkin Family Tomb, Center Cemetery, East Hartford, CT
Fig. 2.9. Memorial Stone Placed by the Friends of Center Cemetery, Inc. listing 16 of Elisha Pitkin's family interred within the tomb, East Hartford, CT
Fig. 3.1. Rediscovered marble tablets identifying the "Tomb of Gershom Bulkeley and his Descendants", Colchester Burying Ground, Colchester, CT
Fig. 3.2. The earthen mound overlying the concealed Gershom Bulkeley Tomb partially uncovered
Fig. 3.3. First view inside the Gershom Bulkeley Tomb
Fig. 3.4. Collapsed coffins with human remains balanced on bottom boards
Fig. 3.5. Drs Albert Harper and State Medical Examiner H. Wayne Carver at the Bulkeley Tomb, Colchester, CT
Fig. 3.6. University of Connecticut graduate student Kristen Bastis at work with Dr Albert Harper sorting through skeletal remains recovered from the Bulkeley Tomb, Colchester, CT

Fig. 3.7. Skeletal remains of Charles Taintor removed from the Bulkeley Tomb for forensic identification
Fig. 3.8. Coffin lid of Gershom's brother, Peter Bulkeley (1712–1798)
Fig. 3.9. Coffin lid of Gershom's son, John Bulkley (1738–1807)
Fig. 3.10. Coffin lid and skeletal remains of Rhoda Jones Kellogg Bulkeley (1750–1807)
Fig. 3.11. Schematic of the interior of the Gershom Bulkeley Tomb showing their original coffin placements
Fig. 3.12. Gold and porcelain dental partials from the burial of Epaphroditus Bulkeley (1791–1817)
Fig. 3.13. Morgan Gardiner Bulkeley (1837–1922)
Fig. 3.14. Right femur of unidentified adult male *in situ* from the Bulkeley Tomb showing severe distal fracture
Fig. 3.15. Coffin hardware handle in situ as recovered from the Bulkeley Tomb
Fig. 3.16. Bulkeley descendants and friends attend reburial ceremony, 11 October 2003
Fig. 3.17. Restored tomb of the Gershom Bulkeley and his Descendants, Colchester Burial Ground, Colchester, CT
Fig. 3.18. Engraved tombstone with names of Bulkeley ancestors identified within the Gershom Bulkeley Tomb)
Fig. 4.1. His Excellency, Samuel Huntington, Esq.
Fig. 4.2. The Tomb of Samuel and Martha Huntington, Norwichtown Cemetery, Norwich, CT, prior to restoration in 2003
Fig. 4.3. Marble epitaph, exterior south wall of the Huntington Tomb
Fig. 4.4. The interior of the Huntington Tomb showing two horizontal rows of stone slabs used to support coffins
Fig. 4.5. Lateral view of the Huntington Tomb (facing east) showing the front façade collapsing from the body of the tomb
Fig. 4.6. Declaration of Independence with Samuel Huntington's signature highlighted
Fig. 4.7. The ribbon tied in a bow on the remains of Martha Huntington
Fig. 4.8. The brass nameplate of His Excellency Governor Samuel Huntington
Fig. 4.9. The brass nameplate of Martha Huntington
Fig. 4.10. Huntington Tomb restoration process, front wall removed
Fig. 4.11. The Governor's First Foot Guard carrying the period coffin of Samuel Huntington during reburial in the Huntington Tomb
Fig. 4.12. The new period coffin of Samuel Huntington returned to the stone shelf, interior, Huntington Tomb
Fig. 4.13. Samuel Huntington Tomb restoration
Fig. 5.1. The Alsop-Chauncey-Mütter Mausoleum, Indian Hill Cemetery, Middletown, CT
Fig. 5.2. Charles Chauncy (1594–1672), Second President of Harvard College
Fig. 5.3. John L. Stephens, William Aspinwall, Henry Chauncey, Panamanian Railroad Owners

List of Illustrations

Fig. 5.4.   The *SS Henry Chauncey*
Fig. 5.5.   Burial vaults on the interior back wall of the Chauncey Tomb
Fig. 5.6.   Interior of the Chauncey Tomb floor after vandalism
Fig. 5.7.   Lower limb skeletal elements, boot of Charles Chauncey (5 years of age) thrust aside on the marble-tiled floor of Chauncey mausoleum
Fig. 5.8.   The inferior portion of Lucy Chauncey's wooden coffin showing skeletal elements of the lower limbs within her burial vault
Fig. 5.9.   Cast-iron coffin and autopsied skull plate of Henry Chauncey as found inside the Chauncey Tomb
Fig. 5.10. Lower volcanized rubber dentures fitting the mandible of Henry Chauncey
Fig. 6.1.   Clay Palo Mayombe pot with 20 sticks protruding around the rim
Fig. 6.2.   Edwin Denison Morgan (1811–1883)
Fig. 6.3.   Back side of Edwin Denison Morgan's Fifth Avenue Mansion and garden viewed from 37th Street
Fig. 6.4.   Westside view of the Edwin Morgan Tomb, Cedar Hill Cemetery, Hartford, CT
Fig. 6.5.   Exposed cast-iron coffin (Burial 1652) of Edwin Denison Morgan in his burial vault
Fig. 6.6.   Exposed wooden coffin (Burial 1314) of Mary B.P. Morgan in her burial vault
Fig. 6.7.   CT Scan images of Mary B.P. Morgan and Edwin Denison Morgan
Fig. 6.8.   A transverse section of the terracotta pot demonstrating brain in the base of skull
Fig. 6.9.   Three-dimensional reconstruction with an algorithm applied to demonstrate metallic artifacts
Fig. 6.10. Wooden stake positioned in front of the skull with feathers adhering
Fig. 6.11. Cluster of artifacts, including rooster skull and wax candle recovered from clay pot
Fig. 6.12. Interior of clay vessel showing white chalk crosses and two horseshoes
Fig. 6.13. Edwin Denison Morgan III (1854–1933)
Fig. 6.14. Edwin Dennison Morgan III's Centerboard Schooner Constellation, 1892
Fig. 6.15. Facial reconstruction of Mary B.P. Morgan from craniofacial remains

Acknowledgements

To acknowledge all the people who assisted us on these tomb projects and in the writing of this book is an enjoyable, but daunting, process. Our hopes are that we have not excluded anyone deserving. Of special note in their contributions to this book are Brian Meyer, who organized all the images, compiled the index, and assembled photographic permissions; Bill Keegan, who developed the map of Connecticut tombs; James "Jim" Hall and Kristen Bastis, whose editorial skills have improved the written context immeasurably. Jim Hall also compiled the glossary at the end of the book. Their combined talents have made this work far better than my abilities to organize and write.

Also, special thanks to Betty Spaulding for permission to use her late husband John's extensive photographic library of our projects. Appreciations to Collin Harty for his design creativity and permission to use the schematic illustrations of the Pitkin and Bulkeley Tomb interiors and Ruth Shapleigh Brown, Executive Director of the Connecticut Gravestone Network, for her counsel over the years on all aspects of historical cemeteries and her support and review of this work.

Assisting us and freely giving of their time and expertise on each of these field projects are:

Moseley Tomb:
Dr Karl Stofko, Ken and Bonnie Beatrice, Anita Sherman, Dave Cooke, June Cooke, John Spaulding, Alison Guinness, Dick LaRose, Ruth Shapleigh-Brown.

Pitkin Family Tomb:
Dave Cooke, John Spaulding, Dick LaRose, Ruth Shapleigh-Brown, Doris Suessman, East Hartford Historical Society, Town of East Hartford Public Works, Friends of Center Cemetery, Inc., Ray Tubbs, Don Pitkin, Ray Johnson, and Dr Albert B. Harper.

Gershom Bulkeley Tomb:
Connecticut Gravestone Network, Dr Albert B. Harper, Dr H. Wayne Carver III, Colchester Municipal Historian Stanley Moroch, Colchester Historical Society, Town of Colchester Public Works, Colchester First Selectwoman Jenny Contois, Arthur Liverant, Peter Bass, Ken and Bonnie Beatrice, Kristen Bastis, Dave Cooke, June Cooke, John Spaulding, Dick LaRose, Peter Bulkeley, Susan Bulkeley Daly, Roger Thompson,

Paul Scannell, Friends of the Office of State Archaeology, Inc., Sven Johnson, George Kinsella, Dr Henri "Hank" Coppes, Ruth Shapleigh-Brown, David Oat, Anita Sherman, Rene Petruzelli, Jackie Nadeau, Kristy Dahlstrom, and Luci Fernandes.

Samuel and Martha Huntington Tomb:

Bill Stanley, Norwich Historical Society, Cara Roure, Mark Macauda, Dave Cooke, Dick LaRose, John Spaulding, Roger Thompson, Paul Scannell, Ivan Myjer, Mark Helmboldt, Church and Allen Funeral Home, Friends of the Office of State Archaeology, Inc., and Channing M. Huntington II.

Chauncey Tomb:

Nancy Wilson, Sgt Relford "Mitch" Ward, Middletown Police Department, Augustus "Augie" DeFrance, Dave Cooke, and Dick LaRose.

Edwin Denison Morgan Tomb:

Molly Rathbun, Dr Richard Gonzalez, Gerald "Jerry" Conlogue, Dr Tania Grgurich, Dr Jaime Ullinger. Dr James Gill, Mary Catherine Sonntag, Michelle Clark, Lucy Freeman, Ruth Shapleigh-Brown, Bill Griswold, Bill Griffith, and Sheila Lafferty.

Gratitude goes out to Julie Gardiner, my editor at Oxbow Books, for her willingness to publish our accounts and for her editorial guidance and, to Jessica Scott, of Oxbow, who saw us through the technical aspects of publication. I thank them for their patience and professionalism.

My heartfelt gratitude to the late David G. Cooke, an amateur archaeologist from Rocky Hill, CT, who was by my side during all but one of these tomb projects and John J. Spaulding, who photo-documented all of our projects for over a decade and provided essential archival work on each of the tomb projects; and, my father Frank known affectionately in the family as "Cheech", who gifted me with the love of history. I miss them every day and this book is dedicated to their memories.

Finally, to my wife Angela, who has been nothing but supportive of all my book projects. Unless you have gone through the process of writing and publishing, it is hard to appreciate the sacrifices that your family makes seeing you through to the final production. None of this could have been accomplished without her unselfish devotion to my work. *La amerò per sempre!*

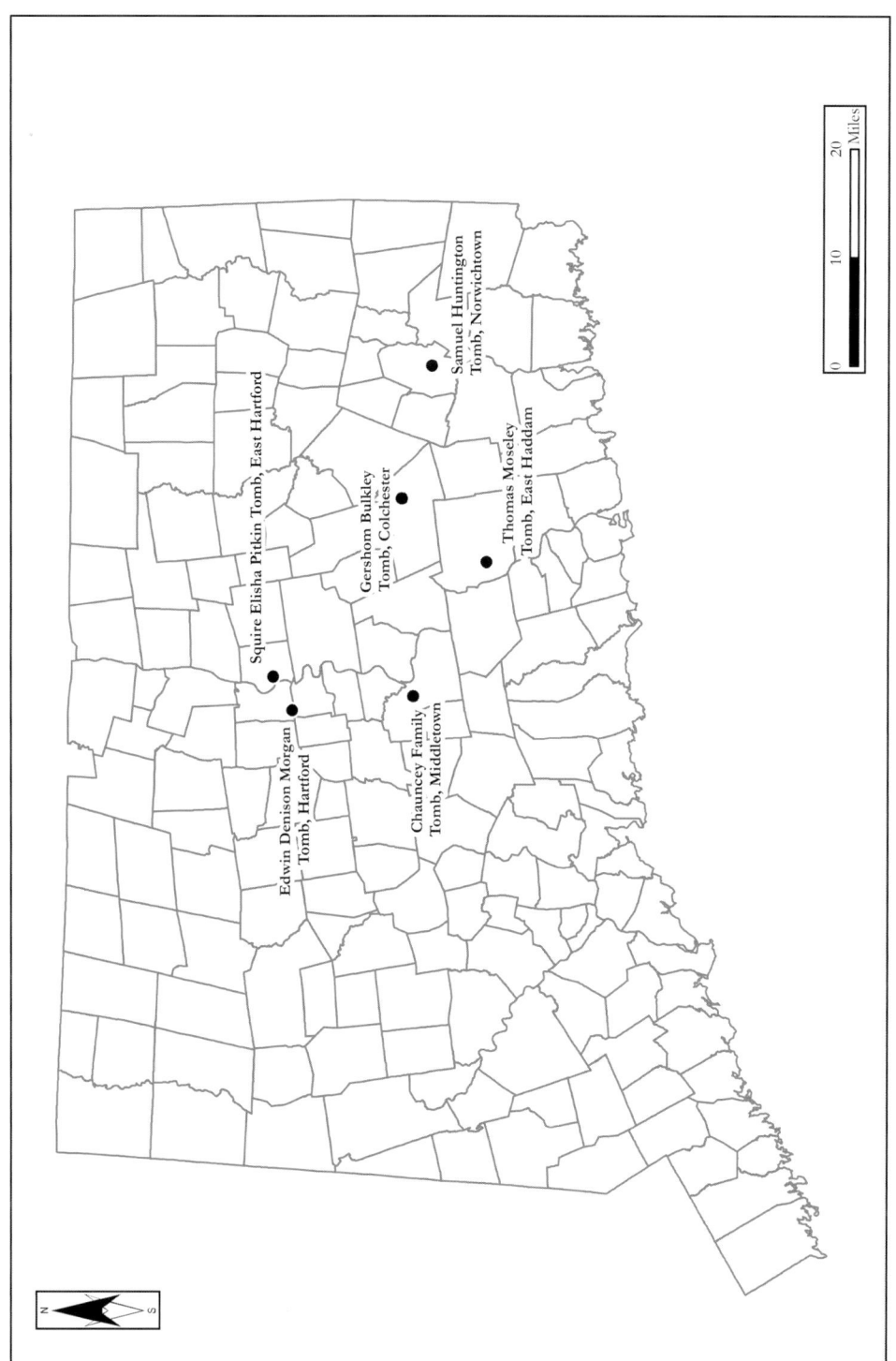

Map 1. Map of the State of Connecticut showing locations of the six family tombs explored in this book (Map by Bill Keegan).

PART I

Tomb Restorations

Chapter 1

Introduction: The Moseley Tomb

And so the tomb remained
Untouched, untended, crumbling, weather-stained.

Thomas Hardy, *The Obliterate Tomb*

The rusted iron door serving as the sole entrance into the age-old Moseley Family Tomb was practically immovable. We pried its tarnished handle hoping the corroded metal would not snap off in our hands. With effort, the oxidized hinges creaked, opening just enough space to wedge my body sideways over the threshold. Entering the tomb, my eyes slowly adjusted to the darkness though I could only discern my shadow cast against the stone of the interior chamber by what morning light seeped through the narrow opening behind me. Unable to distinguish the tomb's contents, I called for a lamp and thrust my arm out the tight entry to receive it. With the beacon balanced on my shoulder, the dusky interior came into sight.

As the Connecticut State Archaeologist, I had been requested to enter the Moseley Family Tomb at East Haddam's First Congregational Church Cemetery to conduct forensic analyses of skeletal remains during the vault's structural restoration, which was necessitated due to extensive water damage, vandalism and collapse of building stones. Constructed by Dr Thomas Moseley, a local physician, in 1790, to repose the remains of his immediate family, the tomb was assembled from dry-laid granite blocks, arched to keystones and was relatively undersized measuring only 13 ft (3.9 m) in length and 10 ft (3.0 m) in width, though at least 8 ft (2.4 m) at its domed peak (Fig. 1.1). The interior walls were whitewashed though now dulled by degradation and time. After 200 years, the weathered tomb was in danger of collapsing, galvanizing the East Haddam Historical Society to raise restoration funds. In light of the rebuilding project, Moseley family descendants granted permission for me to enter the tomb to conduct forensic identifications of their forbearers.

The family was particularly interested in determining whether the ancestral remains of Jonathan Ogden Moseley, the only son of Dr Thomas Moseley, were interred in their historic family burial chamber. Jonathan had served in the Ninth and seven succeeding United States Congresses from Connecticut's At-Large District

Fig. 1.1. Restored Moseley and Gates/Troop Family Tombs, First Church Cemetery, East Haddam, Connecticut. Moseley Tomb is right background (Photo: Brian Meyer).

(1805–1821) as a Federalist (United States Congress nd). Upon leaving Congress, Rep. Moseley moved to his son's new residence in Saginaw, Michigan, in the recently settled Northwest Territory where he died on 9 September 1838 while still practicing law at the age of 77 (Dexter 1911, 153–4). The Library of Congress has no burial record for Rep. Moseley hence the contemporary family had no knowledge as to whether he was interred in Michigan, where there was no headstone, or if his body was brought back to the family tomb in Connecticut.

With the lamp balanced on my shoulder, I surveyed the tomb's somber interior. Before me lay a jumbled mass of fragmented wooden coffins and commingled human skeletal remains littering the floor. Pine coffins had been stacked along the side and back walls, one atop the other as family members were entombed. Through time, the desiccating softwood sideboards failed, tumbling bodies and mortuary hardware onto the dirt floor.

As I scanned the scene, the light from the lamp illuminated a human skull lying on its right side facing me. Even from the distant reflection, I could perceive morphological features suggesting that the cranium (part of the skull that includes the face, upper jaw and the various bones that surround the brain case) represented an older adult male of European ancestry, a choice candidate for the elderly Congressman.

1. Introduction: The Moseley Tomb

Wishing to examine the cranium more closely, I deliberately worked my way toward the back of the tomb careful not to step on any skeletal remains strewn on the floor. As I proceeded deeper into the tomb my lamp cast dark shadows, revealing additional skeletons and coffins, but my interest was focused on the skeletal face peering at me. Bending my knees and crouching over the skull, I reached out to hold it in my hands for closer examination. My extended fingers were within 2 inches of the cranial vault when it started to move, to sway! The skull began to roll slowly side-to-side as if my fingers possessed an energy that brought it to life.

"I've never seen that before," I thought to myself a bit bewildered. And, just as I was mentally searching for a rational explanation for the cranium's sudden movement, a mouse sprang out of the skull! I sucked in air and with a professional and scientific demeanor cried, "EEEEEEWOW!!!"

The base of the skull contains a large hole called the foramen magnum (literally, large hole) through which the spinal cord enters the brain, providing the surprised rodent with an emergency exit as I loomed over it. The terrified mouse was frantically flitting back and forth about skeletal elements and coffin fragments while I pulled air into my depleted lungs. Both our hearts skipped a beat over our sudden encounter.

My colleagues outside the tomb heard the embarrassing shriek and were concerned, anxiously speculating on what had happened to me inside the tomb. So, a bit unsteadily, I rose and slid my body back through the restricted opening to reassure them that I was all right. I mentioned my interest in the skull and the mouse that surprised me. Everyone laughed, though I did not see the humor. One of the masons working on the restoration of the stone tomb, a young man with bulging muscles and crew-cut hair, leaned toward me and asked, "Are you afraid of mice?"

"Hey, give me a break," I cried. "It came out of the skull in a dark tomb while I was reaching for it." Regrettably, my attempted explanation only elicited further laughter, so realizing that my manhood had been challenged I composed myself and reluctantly re-entered the tomb.

Piercing the darkness once more, I relocated the skull and ventured toward it a second time, once again sidestepping any of the dispersed skeletal remains scattered on the tomb floor. I nervously crouched down, put the lamp on the floor and lifted the skull, cradling the cranial vault carefully within my fingers and palms. In doing this, I remembered thinking to myself, "This is heavier than it should be." And, as I did, two more mice jumped out of the skull while it was in my grasp! I shuddered, but held my composure this time and, as calmly as I could, replaced the skull on the floor and exited the crypt. I had had enough.

The mice, it turns out, were using the empty cranial vault as a nest tightly packing the interior of the skull with leaves and twigs for bedding and winter warmth, thus its unexpected heaviness. At this point, I felt like I had three mice roistering round in *my* head.

Subsequent forensic investigation of the tomb's human contents suggested that the skull with the mice may not have been Rep. Jonathan Ogden Moseley, as I originally assumed, but rather, his father, Dr Thomas Moseley, who died at 80 years of age and had built the tomb. Nonetheless, based on forensic techniques and the Moseley family genealogy, the Congressman's remains were confidently identified amid the tomb's scattered skeletons. Shipping his dead body from Michigan in the 1830s would have required a method of preservation before embalming techniques were common in the United States.

The day following our incident with the mice and during lunch break, University of Connecticut students and volunteers from the Friends of the Office of State Archaeology, Inc., who were assisting in the recording of the tomb's contents, presented me with a small gift box wrapped in colorful paper held by a bright ribbon and tied bow. They wanted to give me something they felt I would need in my future tomb investigations. I put down my lunch and gratefully opened the package, revealing two mousetraps.

Published in 1920, Thomas Hardy's poem, *The Obliterate Tomb*, appears to have been composed to describe his wife Emma's sadness in seeing her ancestor's mausoleum being marred during the crypt's attempted restoration. Having been left "untended, crumbling, weather-stained," restoration efforts removed stones which her "grand and great grandparents had put up in years gone by over their vaults, and wept and reflected upon" its demolition (Armstrong 2018). Hardy not only laments tombs that are "doomed to disappear", but that the names of the deceased will be "wiped out in passing years."

> *By these late years their names,*
> *Their virtues, their hereditary claims,*
> *May be as near defacement as their grave place*
> *As are their fames.*

The Moseley Tomb was one of over a dozen "untended, crumbling, weather-stained" burial chambers I have entered in my tenure as the Connecticut State Archaeologist, a position I held for almost 30 years. My entries into historic tombs were for purposes of contemporary restoration projects, criminal vandalism and, sometimes, even at the request of families wishing forensic identification of "lost" ancestors. In fact, I suppose one of my claims to fame, or should I say infamy, is having worked inside more *Obliterated Tombs* than anyone in New England, and possibly in all of America.

Stone and brick tombs were repositories for the physical remains of many wealthy and influential New England families. Their desire may have been to be interred in burial vaults rather than have their wooden coffins laid into the earth in direct contact with crushing soil burden. Hence, prominent families would construct large chambers burrowed into the sides of hills as places of interment for their dead. These are readily seen today dominating the landscape in many historical cemeteries throughout New England.

In contrast, many families of lesser substantial means could hardly afford the expense of an engraved tombstone, let alone an *Obliterate Tomb*, resulting in numerous unmarked graves within our ancient burying grounds becoming lost and often requiring geophysical techniques like ground-penetrating radar to relocate them (Doolittle and Bellantoni 2010). The majority of New England family tombs were built during and immediately after the American Revolution, persisting in modified form into the 21st century. Over time, many of the older structures have begun to collapse after centuries of neglect; some have even become lost, disappearing from sight and contemporary public memory.

That a tomb could simply disappear within a historic cemetery is hard to imagine. Old tombstones can be easily uprooted and moved and, unfortunately, many have been, but tomb structures seem rather permanent. Yet, they have vanished more frequently than you might think. Some were deliberately buried over with earthen berm to conceal their locations from potential vandals (see Chapter 3), while others were dismantled due to cemetery relocations. Some have lost their family identifications (see Chapter 2), or were never noticeably marked, so that the death houses of once prominent people in the community have been completely "lost to history" due to lack of recordkeeping, natural weathering and deliberate concealment.

Regrettably, our work inside extant tombs has also involved coordination with municipal and state police departments when vandals have violated them. Breaking into aged tombs is a relatively easy way to recover skeletal remains prescribed for occult and healing rituals (see Chapters 5 and 6) or collecting memorabilia off the dead for profit; much easier than having to dig through 6 ft of hard-packed earth. As part of crime scene investigations, we have entered tombs to record spatial positioning, conduct forensic examination of skeletal remains, match bone elements removed by vandals and research the uses of skeletal anatomy by occult proponents to better understand their motives and ritualistic requirements. Upon completion of the investigations, we also provided assistance in organizing the reburial of the displaced deceased back into their respective vaults.

Our involvement is the result of Connecticut General Statutes providing roles and responsibilities to the Office of State Archaeology pertaining to unmarked burials. Section 10-388 *et. seq.*, enacted in 1990, defines the roles of the Office of the State's Chief Medical Examiner and the State Archaeologist when human skeletal remains are encountered during construction, agricultural, archaeological or other ground disturbances. The law requires the reporting of any human remains uncovered in any capacity since they could represent modern-day homicides or missing persons. Should the remains be identified as "historical" (50 years old or more) and not part of a recent criminal investigation, the State Archaeologist assumes management of the investigation. While *in situ* preservation is the primary goal, most cases require sensitive archaeological excavation, analysis and reburial of human remains according to the cultural prescriptions of the individual(s) involved (Poirier and Bellantoni 1997). The State Archaeologist is entrusted to oversee analyses, including identification of biological and cultural affiliation as well as contacting descendants, when determined. In every case, a contemporary family, church, Native American tribe, or other affiliated organization represents the dead and assists in decision-making for final disposition of the human remains encountered. As a result of these legislative actions, we have worked with cemetery associations, descendant family, police departments, municipalities and historical societies whenever we have had to enter the state's historic family tombs.

****

When British Puritans settled along the New England shoreline in the early 17th century, they arrived without a well-established tradition of engraved tombstones, let alone construction of mausoleums. In medieval Europe, only the nobility and wealthiest were buried with identification markers, usually crypts consisting of coffin shaped stone coverings beneath or within churches (Ludwig 1999). The graves of commoners went basically unmarked. Nonetheless, in preparation for death, the dying would often appeal to friends and relatives to have their remains buried adjacent to a church. The desire was to be interred *ad santo*, or near the saints, whose sacred relics were often contained in the church's altar. Saints were the only people known to be in heaven, so it was trusted that being buried in immediate proximity to the church would elicit the saint's support in progressing the deceased through the Pearly Gates. With so many burials associated with urban churches, corrosive quicklime was often applied to the corpses to hasten decomposition and reduce the stench, especially during periods of plague. In time, churchyards gained their reputation as bone yards.

By the age of Shakespeare, due to centuries of unmarked burials haphazardly dug into churchyards, space for new interments became extremely limited. As a result, additional graves frequently disturbed the remains of those previously laid in the ground. Remember Hamlet? While digging Ophelia's grave, he encounters the skull of "poor Yorick," the court jester, who had died months before and was buried in the churchyard without a marker. Unintentionally, Hamlet encounters and recognizes Yorick's skull lamenting that he "knew him well." Hamlet's experience would have resonated with Shakespeare's audience.

Due to these increasing burial violations, pious people began to question the sanctity of the grave. Christian theology calls for interment of the dead in a manner that would allow their bodies to remain intact in preparation for the Day of Resurrection when Christ will rise with the morning sun out of the east and remove the faithful from their entombment, joining bodily into eternal salvation. Hence, for the most part, historical Christian burials in New England were laid out in an west-east orientation, head to the west, so the deceased faced the east prepared to meet the rising Christ. If the remains of the dead were inadvertently disrupted and their bones scattered due to subsequent excavation of new graves, would they be able to share in the bliss of the Resurrection? So, increasingly, families started to mark the graves of their loved ones by placing a simple, unaltered stone over the plot, as if to say, "Someone is already buried here, dig elsewhere!"

Engraved tombstones were still uncommon when the English arrived in New England during the early 1600s. In their rebellion against "papist" practices, Puritans at first rejected churchyard burials as being heretical and idolatrous. So, instead of *ad santo* interments, many 17th-century New England townships set aside common land as community burial grounds, while numerous colonial farmers, complaining about difficulty of travel during the winter, frequently buried their families in the backyard. Grave markers back then may have included wooden crosses or unaltered fieldstones many of which have not survived. Ironically, today when we see an old cemetery behind a Congregational Church in New England, often the cemetery was there first with the church built later (Ludwig 1999, 54). The earliest extant burial monument in Connecticut is associated with the Rev. Ephraim Huit (d. 1644) in Palisado Cemetery, Windsor, behind the town's First Congregational Church (Fig. 1.2). Although Rev. Huit was buried in the mid-17th century, his existing monument was most likely constructed at a later, 18th century, date and an accompanying memorial epitaph in 1842.

Fig. 1.2. Earliest dated burial marker in Connecticut, 1644, Rev. Huit, Palisado Cemetery, Windsor, Connecticut (Photo: Brian Meyer).

To the Puritan, death could be viewed as either a reward or a punishment. Only the "elect" would experience the bliss of heaven, while others would sustain the punishment of hell and, since no one could be sure of being among the elect, there was a sense of insecurity and ambivalence (Stannard 1977), leaving funerals empty of ceremony and with a restraint on emotions. It was not until the late 17th and early 18th centuries that we witness the familiar iconographic tombstones characteristic of historic New England burying grounds (Fig. 1.3). Winged soul effigies, skulls and crossbones (*memento mori*), and hourglasses (*hora fugit*) become reoccurring themes that stone carvers used to emphasize the fleetingness of this world and the need to prepare for final judgment and eternity. Based on English traditions, these tombstones also call out for the triumph of death and the new life that death provides in eternity (Ludwig 1999, 77).

When visiting the grave of a loved one in colonial New England, you were not only paying your respects to the dead, but you were confronting your own mortality. Be prepared to answer to a "judgmental" God where eternal damnation may await you. One East Hartford, Connecticut, epitaph warns,

> *Death is a Debt to Nature Due*
> *Which I have Paid, and So Must You.*

Fig. 1.3. Classic 18th-century iconographic New England headstone (Photo: Brian Meyer).

The 19th century produced religious revitalizations that induced more peaceful images of death and judgment as viewed from a loving and merciful God. The Great Awakenings and their waves of religious enthusiasm offered a more optimistic attitude toward death (Stannard 1975, 143). Eternal rest was viewed as a just reward for a pious life. A divine, loving and compassionate "Father" judges based on personal merit rather than inherited sins and is prepared to bestow His benevolence on those that have been faithful. Weeping willows, trees of life, flowers and Classical Grecian urns predominate, while carved images and marble headstones are relatively plain. A Killingly, Connecticut, epitaph simply reads, "She Did The Best She Could." Nothing fancy with a modicum of iconography.

Exclusive family vaults, sometimes chamber tombs built to hold 30 or more individuals, were primarily constructed with relatively abundant brick, brownstone and granite in early New England, and saw their rise around the time of the American Revolution. Prior to the 20th century, and at times even after, documentation of the tomb's denizens was often non-existent, so that even burials of our most prominent citizens remained unknown. Think of Congressman Jonathan Ogden Moseley.

The "rural" cemetery movement in the 1840s marked the beginning of major changes in the burial place by initiating the concept of suburban park-like aesthetic landscapes permitting cemetery visitors the opportunity of communing with their deceased loved ones, picnicking and driving carriages along tranquil winding roads amid monuments, lawns, ponds, wildlife, planted exotic trees and shrubbery. Instead of pallbearers carrying the coffin to the nearby burying ground, carriages, or hearses, were specifically designed to convey the coffin to suburban settings with elaborate ornamental features (McRae 2004, 31). This prettification program even lead to changes in nomenclature: before the mid-19th century, the dead were interred in "burying grounds;" afterward, they were laid to rest in "cemeteries", a sleeping place (Llewellyn 1998, 24), a beautiful space of landscaped architecture and spectacular views (McRae 2004, 32).

The corresponding "City Beautiful" movement of the mid-19th century concerned itself in part with the lack of parks within urban areas which, proponents believed, steered people to congregate in the open spaces of burial grounds, further leading to cemetery vandalism and the disruption of tombstones. The need for more parks and outlying cemeteries designed for the proper care of graves was deemed essential (Anon. 1903, 9). In addition, city cemeteries were considered "unsanitary" and it was thought to be socially inappropriate to have a graveyard at the center of a thriving industrial, urban community (McRae 2004, 30).

These concerns initiated the spread of a "planned cemetery" outside the city limits with "perpetual care" and the "depersonalization" of the burial plot, which encouraged management by professionals and eliminated the need for family cemetery visits to maintain the grave (Jackson 1977, 310). The first planned cemetery in America was Grove Street Cemetery, incorporated in 1796 in New Haven, Connecticut to replace the old graveyard on the New Haven Green in the heart of the city. At the time, the privately-owned Grove Street Cemetery was outside the city limits and was laid out in a grid pattern with paths wide enough for carriages to transverse and trees planted throughout (McRae 2004, 31), becoming the model of all others throughout New England.

With the rise of the Industrial Revolution and the creation of an entitled upper socio-economic class, mortuary monuments reached their literal and classical heights while family tombs increased in size and numbers in New England cemeteries, symbolizing in death the status "Gilded Age" elites attained during their earthly lives. The Victorian Era saw the development of colossal mortuary architecture (Fig. 1.4), including Egyptian obelisks reaching for the heavens, elaborate statuary with weeping angels at the tomb's entrance, and grand mausoleums of varying design, some of which contained personal chapels for prayer and contemplation.

By the 1920s, traditional tombstones were becoming standardized, depleted of ornate designs and commonly replaced by ground-level bronze plaques (McRae 2004, 31). Cemetery monuments become increasingly democratized and secular. Instead of flaunting wealth and social status, the emerging middle-class desired grave markers that simply listed the surname of the dead on an unadorned stone. No epitaph or moral religious message was required since cemeteries were to be "cheerful places"

Fig. 1.4. Cedar Hill Cemetery, "Rural" Cemetery Movement, marble burial monument of Samuel Colt in center, Hartford, Connecticut (Photo: Brian Meyer).

(Tilton 1908, 22). As 20th-century American life shifted from a world of family and community ties to one of constant mobility due to industrialized transportation and changing workplaces and social structures tied to non-relatives, cemetery maintenance responsibilities also shifted to superintendents and funeral directors (Stannard 1980, 28), and away from individual families, whose members may no longer live in areas where their ancestors were buried.

Many years ago, I interviewed a memorial stone carver inquiring what people requested for monuments and was told that they invariably asked, "What do other families do?" Conformity and simplicity ruled as families, in their grief, simply complied with what other families were doing, not wanting to be exceptional. Renowned actress Katherine Hepburn's family tombstone at Cedar Hill Cemetery in Hartford, Connecticut is made from unfinished granite discretely hidden behind shrubbery and is simply inscribed with the family's surname (Fig. 1.5). One has to search the ground for the bronze marker of Katherine's plot. There is nothing noticeable that pronounces the Hepburn family's wealth or prestige. You can easily walk by without ever noticing the stone.

Fig. 1.5. The family tombstone of actress Katherine Hepburn, Cedar Hill Cemetery, Hartford, Connecticut (Photo: Brian Meyer).

The early 20th century elaborated on the "rural" cemetery concept in the development of "Memorial Parks" (Llewellyn 1998, 28). Envisioned by Hubert L. Eaton in 1917, Memorial or Lawn Parks were cemeteries conceived with the idea that the spiritual and inspirational representation of deceased loved ones was more important than the physical embodiment of burial monuments. Grave markers were simple and lay flat on the ground. Uninterrupted open spaces with trees and expansive lawns were to provide reflection and religious experience. Forest Lawn Memorial Park in Glendale, California is one of the first and primary examples of Eaton's idea; many others were to follow, including Rose Hill Cemetery, Rocky Hill, Connecticut.

In the 21st century, technology-driven computer imaging has allowed tombstones to become once again more personalized. No longer engraved by hand, tombstones can be etched by computerized diamond-tipped drill bits onto polished black granite with an extraordinary degree of precision, generating artistic imagery of personal life stories. Some modern tombstones have Quick Response (QR) Codes allowing the visitor to scan with their smartphones and link to websites sharing photographs, eulogies, genealogies and videos creating digital records of the decease's existence (Reeson 2015). The Pitkin Tomb (see Chapter 2; Fig. 1.6) has signage by the front entrance with a QR code for the visitor to scan and learn about the colonial Pitkin family and their burial vault.

So, the back-and-forth pattern of mortuary monuments in New England cemeteries straddles an early period where very few preserving markers exist (17th century); to a time where personal, elaborately carved and iconographic tombstones elicited warnings of eternal damnation (18th century); to plain, simple (usually white marble) markers with at best a one-line epitaph emphasizing deserved eternal rest (early 19th century); to monumental mortuary architecture and lovely landscaped vistas for the wealthy (mid-to-late 19th century) symbolizing their upper socioeconomic status; to democratic conformity in an age of great mobility and consumerism (20th century); and, finally, to computer-generated art, personal images and website-linking capabilities of the 21st century. Cemeteries and their burial markers and positions on the cultural landscape manifest technological transformations, but more so, they reveal our changing spiritual and social attitudes. Burying grounds are more than resting places for our dead: They speak to our cultural history.

****

Few people today have ever entered Hardy's *Obliterate Tomb*, much to their personal satisfaction I am sure. But, due to our forensic and archaeological experience, we have been summoned into many old burial chambers. This book covers our entries into five Connecticut tombs, which include the family mausoleums of Squire Elisha Pitkin, Center Cemetery, East Hartford; Gershom Bulkeley, Colchester Burial Ground, Colchester; Samuel and Martha Huntington, Norwichtown Cemetery, Norwich; Henry

Fig. 1.6. Pitkin Tomb Signage with Quick Response (QR) Code Bar, Center Cemetery, East Hartford, Connecticut (Photo: Brian Meyer).

Chauncey, Indian Hill Cemetery, Middletown; and Edwin Denison Morgan, Cedar Hill Cemetery, Hartford. In all of these cases, the State Archaeologist and a team of researchers and volunteers assisted in identifying and restoring human skeletal remains to their original burial placements following vandalism, or contributed to the identification of unrecorded historical burials during restoration projects. The intent of this book is to tell first-hand stories of the State Archaeologist's investigations into these tombs, including family histories and the science behind our work, a subfield called "forensic archaeology."

Forensic Archaeology can be simply defined as a science that employs the application of archaeological principles, techniques and methodologies in a legal context, predominately medico-legal and law enforcement (Blau and Ubelaker 2016, 22). Archaeology, as taught in American universities, is a part of anthropology, so our research goals involve an understanding of past human behavior. Hence, archaeology can be defined as the systematic study of material remains of human behavioral antiquity. Forensic archaeology is the "anthropology of the dead." We ask fundamentally behavioral questions through observational tools and we do this at the individual and group levels (Morse *et al.* 1983).

Archaeologists working within the cultural context of death frame a series of questions about the "How, When, What, Where and Why" of human behavior pertaining to fatality. What are the events leading up to death? What was the cause and manner of death? How are human remains treated before and after death? When and where did death take place? What is the ultimate disposal of the dead individually and/or collectively? Why are the dead treated in the manner observed?

As a result of these research interests, which are similar to questions asked by law enforcement officials when investigating homicides, archaeologists have been called upon to assist in the recovery of material culture and the examination and interpretation of human skeletal remains in criminal or natural disaster cases in many countries around the world. In the United States, for example, forensic archaeologists and anthropologists are included as members of the U.S. government's Disaster Mortuary Operational Response Teams (DMORT) for the Department of Health & Human Services. Disaster mortuary personnel attempt to identify and analyze victims in the field where human life has been affected by natural and cultural catastrophes (Sledzik and Hunt 1997). DMORT cases reflect a wide range of disasters, as from the 9/11 World Trade Center attack in New York City at Ground Zero and at the Staten Island landfill where materials were brought for identification, to Hardin Cemetery, Missouri, where burials were obliterated by floodwaters in 1993, sweeping away 769 bodies that necessitated reconstruction and identification (Sledzik and Hunt 1997, 185–198).

Forensic archaeologists also play a role in the investigations of human rights violations around the world where mass burials of political and ethnic groups are involved (U.S. Department of Health and Human Services 2020), especially when all that may remain of the victims are unidentified skeletal remains. In addition, scientists and historians are working to research the last known locations of military personnel with hopes of identifying and bringing the remains of MIAs home. The U.S. Department of Defense maintains a database of soldiers missing in action through the Armed Forces DNA Identification Laboratory in Hawaii in hopes of recovering and distinguishing skeletal remains discovered in former war zones. Forensic archaeology/anthropology has become an integral part of crime scene investigations and many medical examiner offices around the country currently employ forensic anthropologists/archaeologists as staff members.

Crime scene investigation and archaeology share many methodological components. For example, both processes of data recovery are inherently destructive. In the field, whether a crime scene or an archaeological site, the removal of artifacts (*i.e.*, evidences) without proper recording of spatial context will result in the loss of information that can never be retrieved. If you remove the "bloody glove" from the scene of the crime before proper documentation, its relevance may not be admissible in a court of law. Likewise, if archaeological context is not recorded, you merely recover artifacts (*i.e.*, treasure hunting) without the ability to answer behavioral questions about the human past. Additionally, both methods attempt to reconstruct undocumented events: crimes are clandestine, and none of us were here hundreds or thousands of years ago when the dead were culturally treated in preparation for the next life. So, there is the need for careful 3-dimensional documentation of data, especially for buried victims where recording x, y, and z coordinates are critical to interpretation. Ultimately, both crime scene investigation and archaeology are concerned with spatial analysis and the sequence of events.

I would argue, and have done to law enforcement officials, that archaeological expertise provides a more complete recovery of crime scene information and better documentation of buried physical evidence. Archaeologists are trained to get the most minuscule botanical or bone fragment from the soil in a way that is preserved and valuable for laboratory analyses. Unfortunately, documentation of this nature is time-consuming and often police are under a great deal of pressure to solve crimes expeditiously. So, archaeologists working in real world criminal investigative situations understand that being efficient and timely in our labor is essential. Working together, forensic archaeologists and law enforcement officials, can find the appropriate balance of pace for proper recording while moving criminal cases forward in a sensible fashion. As archaeologists, we are pleased that our particular and peculiar training in understanding mortuary practices of past cultures and our examination of human skeletal remains have a practical application in solving contemporary human problems.

All these tomb studies began either as "history mysteries" or as crime scene investigations, allowing us to venture further into areas of cross-cultural treatment of the dead, changing mortuary technology, landscape architecture, and public health; as well as the activities of occult and Santeria rituals that employ human remains as part of harming and healing ceremonies. Since built burial chambers were occupied by social and economic elites, forensic studies also provide an opportunity to investigate the health and life stress pathologies of the wealthiest citizens in Connecticut's historical past, while offering comparisons to the well-being of lower socio-economic populations. So, we chronicle a timeframe of history, forensic anthropology and archaeology, religious beliefs and family genealogy as aspects of each investigation. And, maybe a personal story thrown in, fortunately no further encounters with mice inhabiting human skulls.

Chapter 2

Squire Elisha Pitkin Family Tomb

No marble tablets, urns, or stones,
Tell where repose their honored bones.
The tide of time, and sure decay
Have swept from memory these away.

A.P. Pitkin, *Pitkin Genealogy*

Historical records can be misleading at times, often requiring a bit of critical reading (and thinking) to determine accurateness. This is what historians do. So, when the 1887 Pitkin genealogy listed 18 family members "placed in the (old) tomb" as having "since been removed and interred in the adjoining ground," archivists assumed the account was accurate, hence believing that the longstanding tomb had been emptied of its human occupants (Pitkin 1887, lxix). On the other hand, only five associated headstones could be identified in the "adjoining ground." What of the other 13 original tomb occupants? Did their earthen graves remain unmarked? Regardless of this discrepancy, the tomb was considered a cenotaph, that is, empty (Spaulding and Bellantoni 2001). They were wrong.

To complicate matters further, no family name or marker appeared on the edifice's façade, leading some 20th-century cemetery historians to wonder if the brick structure really was the longstanding Pitkin Family Tomb, speculating that it was more likely a "receiving or holding vault," constructed to "receive" the corpses of those who died during the winter when deep snow and frozen earth made digging by hand shovels impossible, thus "holding" burials until spring when the ground thawed. Either way, holding vault or cenotaph, no bodies were anticipated to repose within.

The Pitkin Tomb remains a most impressive monument at Center Cemetery, East Hartford, Connecticut, conspicuously standing out along the north-facing slope of high ground above the cemetery's Main Street entrance (Fig. 2.1). It measures 13 ft (3.9 m) wide, 17 ft (5.2 m) in length, and 9 ft (2.7 m) in height. From the Main Street entrance, the brick tomb appears on your left, emerging out of the knoll as you walk up the hill, its domed roof almost touching the ground at the upslope end.

2. Squire Elisha Pitkin Family Tomb

Fig. 2.1. Pitkin Family Tomb, Center Cemetery, East Hartford, Connecticut (Photo: Brian Meyer).

Constructed in the early 1790s by Squire Elisha Pitkin to house the mortal remains of his immediate family and their descendants, the tomb has a brownstone foundation underlying mortared bricks layered to an arching dome. There is no other structure like it within the cemetery.

Since 1723 there have been an astonishing 187 Pitkin family members buried in Center Cemetery, the most recent in 1928 (Spaulding and Bellantoni 2001, 3). Along with the Goodwin family, with whom they intermarried, the Pitkins were beyond doubt the most prominent clan in Hartford's East Side from 1661 to 1850, though few descendants reside in town today. Incorporated as the Town of East Hartford shortly after the Revolutionary War in 1783, a map of Hartford's East Side prior to 1840 lists no fewer than 24 Pitkin residences as well as the Pitkin Fort, situated on the first terrace overlooking the Connecticut River's meadows (Pitkin 1887, lxiii) along the town's first Main Street (today's Prospect Street). The Pitkin Fort was built to provide refuge from Indian attack during King Philip's War in the 1670s. Operating gristmills, stores, wharves, hotels, glass works as well as serving on every colonial town committee, Pitkins literally dominated the East Side politically and economically. Bruce Colin Daniels denotes them as Connecticut Colony's most influential "First Family" (1975, 7).

Ironically, I spent my high school years in East Hartford after our family moved there from the south end of Hartford (Little Italy) in 1963. As a teenager driving down Main Street I often glimpsed the brick-arched tomb on the cemetery hill, but was never curious enough to take a closer look. Of course, back then I was not thinking toward a career in archaeology, so I gave little thought to the vault, except to note that it was an unusual structure and wondered who might be buried in it. Be that as it may, years later, as State Archaeologist, when I received a phone call from

East Hartford municipal historian Doris Suessman concerning a brick roof collapse at a tomb in Center Cemetery I knew the exact mausoleum she referred to.

In 2000, the Friends of Center Cemetery contracted to repair the mortared brick roof of the "empty" vault, which was badly deteriorated and had developed into a safety concern. During the restoration, part of the original brick arch collapsed into the tomb's interior. Eager to assess the damage and determine if the dome needed to be reinforced from the inside, town workmen removed a corroded outer steel plate, exposing the original door and entered the tomb. Rather than being "empty" as all assumed, they found, much to their bewilderment, human skeletal remains strewn amid a number of desiccated wooden and rusted metal coffins. At that point, Doris called for assistance.

The phone call I received told of the roof collapse and the surprising discovery of coffins and skeletons inside the supposedly vacant burial vault. But, even more astonishing, Doris exclaimed, was the presence of an Egyptian sarcophagus in the chamber! "In a historic New England tomb?" I questioned. "I don't think so!" Nevertheless, I told her we would come right out and investigate.

The Egyptian sarcophagus was in reality a Fisk Metallic Burial Case, patented in 1848 by Almond Dunbar Fisk and originally manufactured in Providence, Rhode Island (United States Patent Office 1848). The Fisk Burial Case, unlike hexagonal wooden coffins or rectangular metal caskets, was shaped to conform firmly to human anatomy lying in a supine position: rounded head, extending out to wide shoulders, tapering in to a narrow waist, flaring pelvis and slimming to upward pointing feet (Figs 2.2 and 2.3). A "viewing glass" allowed the face to be seen during the funeral without the need to open the coffin lid, hence minimizing the removal of funerary souvenirs (*i.e.*, hair lockets, etc.) from the dead and guaranteeing the least corruption of the deceased's body in its wait for the Day of Resurrection. A nameplate was situated over the crossed arms at the chest giving identity to the person within. Until this time, I had only seen illustrations of a Fisk Burial Case in historic mortuary catalogues and drawings and had never seen one in an actual burial context. It was certainly unique and I appreciated why they thought it was of ancient Egyptian origin.

The Fisk Metallic Burial Case residing in the tomb was badly oxidized and tightly sealed, so no attempt was made to open it and examine the remains. More importantly, the tarnished nameplate gave identification: *Dr. Edward Pitkin, d. 1851*, providing our first inkling that this was indeed the old Pitkin Family Tomb and that it was certainly not empty.

****

He smiled softly when first discerning her animated eyes through the dim candlelight of the semi-darkened dining hall. He had sailed to America in 1659 with the notion that his visit to the New England Colonies would be short-term as he wished to return to Britain and commence his occupation in law. Her captivating eyes changed William

2. Squire Elisha Pitkin Family Tomb

JAMES R. FISHER,

SEXTON AND

UNDERTAKER

NO. 134 CLARK STREET, NEAR CORNER OF MADISON,

And Retail Agent for the Sale of

FISK'S PATENT METALLIC BURIAL CASES.

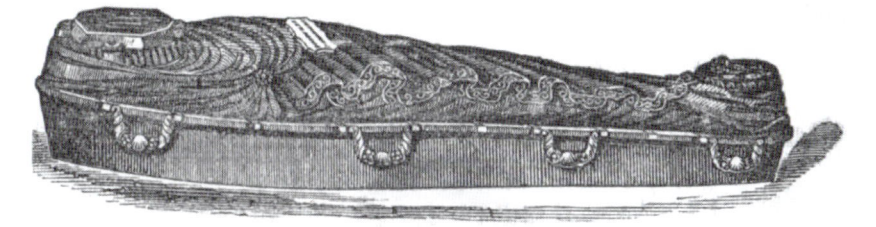

Keeps constantly on hand all descriptions of Rosewood, Mahogany, Black Walnut, and other **COFFINS**. Also, **Shrouds**, and everything requisite for Funerals.

HEARSES AND CARRIAGES FURNISHED,

And all calls attended to by **Day** or **Night**.

Fig. 2.2. A 19th-century advertisement for the Fisk Metallic Burial Case (From The Chicago City Directory and Business Advertiser, Fourth Edition, 1855).

Fig. 2.3. Fisk Metallic Coffin of Dr Edward Pitkin, d. 1851 (left) and the Pulp-Fisk Coffin of his wife Carlissa Pitkin, d. 1876 (right) (Photo: John J. Spaulding).

Pitkin's intentions. During his sojourn in the Connecticut River Valley, young William met and immediately fell in love with Hannah Goodwin, proprietor of those luring brown eyes, in Hartford, marrying her within 2 years and remaining an influential town resident until his death in 1694. William never returned to England (Daniels 1975, 11).

Educated and financially endowed, William "the Immigrant" (as the family would later refer to him) became Hartford's third schoolmaster and served on many public committees. He was also one of the earliest proprietors of the East Side Society (Parish) of Hartford, the land directly across the Connecticut River which consisted of a large treeless meadow, prime for farming, and a high terrace with well-drained soils on which to reside. He became the largest landowner there, owning over 800 acres (ca. 324 ha) bought directly from the heirs of renowned local tribal leader Sachem Uncas of the Mohegans, becoming one of colony's most prominent political figures by the late 17th century (Daniels 1975, 8).

Although not a chartered proprietor of Hartford, William and his family nonetheless proliferated through successive generations, and eventually occupied the majority of houses along the first Main Street of the "East Side." These included three Pitkin inns and the residence of Capt. James Pitkin who commanded the first steamboat up the Connecticut River about 1825 (Goodwin 1879, 230; Pitkin 1887, 36). William and Hannah had eight children, including William, Jr. (The family appears to be enamored with the appellation of "William" since the forename can be extended back to at least William the Immigrant's grandfather in England and would continue, much to the chagrin of New England genealogists, through many succeeding generations in America).

William (2) was enormously influential in his own right. In 1697, 3 years after his father's death, he was elected as an assistant to the Connecticut General Assembly and held one of the most powerful political positions in the colony (Daniels 1975, 17). In the early 18th century William was appointed Judge of the Hartford County Court with his name appearing on all the most important political documents of the time. He married Elizabeth Stanley in 1687 and together they had 11 children, counting (you guessed it) another William (3), the eventual Governor of the Connecticut Colony, and Joseph, who would wed Mary Lord in 1726 and have nine children, including Squire Elisha in 1733. Over 200 Pitkin children would be baptized in the East Side's Third Church of Hartford Congregational (Pitkin 1887). They were a typically large colonial family whose kinship network would create the most powerful political, social and economic name in the Connecticut Colony.

Squire Elisha Pitkin's father, Joseph, was appointed Ensign to the State Militia in 1730 and by 1751 was advanced to full Colonel during the French and Indian War. Though inheriting land and his father's dwelling house, Joseph would fall on hard times due to his involvement in failed land speculations and other unsuccessful business dealings, dying bankrupt in 1762 (Daniels 1975, 40).

Elisha's paternal uncle, William Pitkin (3) served the Connecticut Colony as Governor (1766–1769) during tumultuous times. The First Great Awakening divided the

Congregational Church between Old-Lights, who strived to maintain the traditional Puritan orthodoxy and New-Light revivalists attempting to return the church to its "original" belief. The East Side Pitkins were New-Light advocates and William negotiated the treacherous political/religious waters with diplomacy and was respected by both factions (Daniels 1975, 36). He was elected to the governorship in 1766 and though re-elected three times (Governor's served 1-year terms back then), these were not the happiest of years for William or the Pitkin family. He lost his wife, Mary, during the spring of his first term and he would die while in office at the age of 75 as tensions were developing with the British Monarchy over the Stamp and Townshend Acts. Revolution was at the doorstep.

The fourth generation of Pitkin men came of age during American Revolutionary Connecticut assuming positions of leadership during the war. Squire Elisha (Fig. 2.4) inherited the family duty to serve and would one day be appointed Colonel like his father. When signs of discontent with King George III and the English Parliament escalated in 1770, Elisha Pitkin, ever the Patriot of Independence, was appointed to a committee charged with preventing importation of British goods into Connecticut and, instead, promoting the use of American manufactures (in which he was greatly involved financially). With "the shot heard around the world" echoing out of nearby Concord and Lexington, Massachusetts, Squire Elisha was commissioned "Captain" in the Connecticut State Militia (Pitkin 1887, lxx).

Squire Pitkin was a force to be reckoned with. He was one of the first of his extended family to graduate from Yale College and he served the East Side as a soldier, businessman, magistrate and justice. He evidently had a firm way of administering law, though with a wry sense of humor. When a member of the Evans family, whose clan had a bad reputation in the community, was brought before him on a criminal charge, the Honorable Elisha Pitkin asked the defendant's name. "Evans," was the answer. "Evans?" exclaimed Justice Pitkin without hearing another word. "Guilty, then!" (Goodwin 1879, 229).

East Side proprietors had petitioned the Colony as early as 1726 to have their own church and incorporate as a separate town citing hardships of crossing the Connecticut River to attend religious services and conduct town

Fig. 2.4. Squire Elisha Pitkin (from Pitkin 1887).

business during winter, but the request was not granted until the end of the Revolutionary War. The first official East Hartford town meeting was held on 8 November 1783 with 41 charter officers chosen, 13, or one-third of them, were named Pitkin.

Elisha was appointed East Hartford's representative to the General Assembly, serving from 1784 to 1805. He owned a third of the Pitkin Glass Works, the earliest glass factory in Connecticut, and was also engaged in the manufacturing of gunpowder, snuff and anchors, financially immersing himself in the West Indies Trade. His two-chimney, gambrel-roofed house (Fig. 2.5) was constructed in 1764 with his great-grandfather's original 1690 Dutch ell to the rear (Zimmerman 1979). This residence had so many visitors over the years that it was nicknamed the "Minister's House" due to the large number of clergymen who were entertained there. Elisha was quite the congenial and accommodating host (Goodwin 1879, 145).

Without doubt his most illustrious houseguest was the French General Jean-Baptiste Donatien de Vimeur, comte de Rochambeau, who lodged there twice (Goodwin 1879, 89; Pitkin 1887, 439; Fig. 2.6). From 22–25 June 1781, Rochambeau

Fig. 2.5. House of Squire Elisha Pitkin as it stood in East Hartford, Connecticut (National Register nomination – Zimmerman 1979). (Credit: Historic American Buildings Survey Collection, Library of Congress).

bivouacked his French Army (Camp #6) for an extended 3-day period in the fields less than a mile from Squire Elisha's home in East Hartford. The French Army, 15,000 soldiers strong, was marching inland and westward from Newport, Rhode Island, to rendezvous with General George Washington at the Hudson River Heights. The combined French and Patriot forces would in time defeat British General Charles Cornwallis at Yorktown and secure American Independence.

By the early 1780s, the East Side had grown to such an extent that it was capable of accommodating Rochambeau's divisional headquarters and the army's departments during both their outward and inward marches and still be close enough for political and military leaders to attend meetings in the main city across the Connecticut River. Elisha hosted the French general at his house for the 3-day stay, entertaining his distinguished guest with numerous barrels of soup, roasts and barbecues (Goodwin 1879, 89). Conversations were lively.

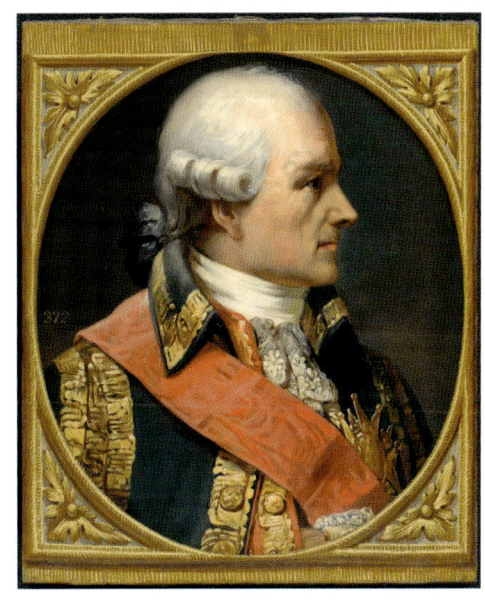

Fig. 2.6. French General Comte de Rochambeau (Credit: National Portrait Gallery, Smithsonian Institution).

Nearby, Elisha's younger brother Richard owned a tavern that was a popular watering hole for the French soldiers. Stories of cattle roasts and late-night dancing were perpetuated for decades afterward. In fact, the entire town benefited greatly during the French stopovers. Attractive American girls were courted and their mothers were paid to sew and bake for the French soldiers; the Meeting House, near Elisha's home, was set up as a hospital and the town was nicely compensated for its use; and Timothy Forbes' residence near the Hockanum River was selected to store barrels of silver coins used to pay the army in his basement (Pitkin 1887). In commemoration, the main road along the fields occupied by the French near Forbes' house is known today as "Silver Lane" (Federal Writer's Project 1938, 440). The French had such a pleasurable time that they happily camped there once again on their victorious return trip in 1782.

As one of the most prominent and prosperous individuals in town, Squire Elisha Pitkin owned African captives. Among these was a woman named Flora, who had a daughter, Tanner, in 1785. When Squire Pitkin died, he left 200 acres (81 ha) of woodland for Tanner's aid. However, "Old Flo" lived to a ripe old age and Elisha's son, Dr Edward Pitkin, who would repose in the Fisk Metallic Burial Case, turned her over to the town for keeping since he had grown weary of supporting her (Goodwin 1879, 234–5).

As Squire Elisha Pitkin approached his 60th year in the early 1790s, his thoughts turned toward the epitaph on the tombstone of his uncle, his Excellency William Pitkin (3). The former governor was laid to rest in Center Cemetery in 1769 with a graphic epitaph warning:

> Walk Thoughtful on the Solemn Shore
> Of that Vast Ocean Thou Art Soon to Pass

Though Elisha would not "pass" that vast ocean until 1819 at the ripe old age of 86, he purchased a triangular piece of land from Joseph Goodwin on property that abutted the northerly border of Center Cemetery and there he prepared to build a granite and brick tomb near his uncle's grave substantial enough to house his mortal remains and those of his rapidly developing family (Goodwin 1879, 115).

****

During a public presentation on Colonial mortuary practices, I joked to the audience that I had already selected the epitaph for my tombstone, which will read: *I Knew This Would Happen Some Day!* The subsequent, nervous laughter acknowledged that we all face the certainty of death, no matter how much we may wish to prolong it.

Anthropologists refer to "death" as one of the ultimate problems of human existence. Answering questions surrounding death and providing appropriate responses (*i.e.*, ritual) is one of the significant roles of religion within a cultural framework. The religious system of every culture defines the meaning of death, establishes suitable periods of mourning, and guides the physical treatment of human remains, as well as providing spiritual explanations of the afterlife.

In addition, each death creates a social vacuum. When a political, religious, or business leader passes; when a farmer, carpenter, or laborer leaves us; when a father, mother, son or daughter dies their varied roles require replacement for society to continue to function. The cultural response to death goes beyond the everyday practical necessity of adapting to the physical world around us. To humans, death requires spiritual explanation and corporeal ritual.

There is some evidence to suggest that Neanderthals were the earliest peoples to, occasionally, deliberately bury their dead with some ceremony (Solecki 1975) but it is not until the Neolithic period (New Stone Age) that formal burials in monumental tombs appear. In western Europe the practice of constructing long earthen and stone burial mounds is one diagnostic aspect accompanying the change from a mobile hunter-gatherer existence to a more sedentary lifestyle and the Agricultural Revolution of the period (ca 5500–2500 BCE). Like the tombs discussed here, these long mounds contained multiple burials but generally they exhibit little social differentiation between individuals and it is often clear that these ancestors were revisited and their bones moved around, with new burials being added later (Cunliffe

2001; Bickle *et al.* 2017). More elaborate tombs were constructed during later periods, though there was a major change, in many parts of Europe, to individual burials, often with grave goods, and the practice of cremation and burial with pottery vessels in round mounds (barrows or tumuli). In North America, Hopewell and Adena Cultures, for example, developed elaborate mound burials in the Ohio and Mississippi River Valleys beginning over 2000 years ago (Woodward and McDonald 2002; Lynott 2015).

During the subsequent "Rise of Civilization" between 4000 and 3000 BCE in the Middle East we witness truly differential treatment of the dead in human society. Divine and semi-divine kings and their royal families were provided elaborate enshrinement within monumental architecture designed to hold their remains and symbolize their elite social and deified status in death. Commoners, usually farmers, peasants and slaves were buried with no monuments and wherever bodies could be disposed, sometimes within caves. The roots of human inequality were literally "rooted" in the differential disposition of the dead.

"Tomb" is loosely interpreted to mean any kind of burial house for the dead, above or below ground. In many early cultures the dead were often buried directly underneath their houses, so the original concept of a tomb may have been derived from "a house for the dead," reproducing primitive dwelling types. Often accompanying the dead were tools, weapons and personal effects indispensable in the next life. With the rise of social elites, the concept of placing material goods in the graves with the deceased was extended to include human servants and slaves, who were put to death in order to serve their masters for eternity. China's first Qin emperor, Qin Shi Huang, who unified the country, was buried (ca. 210 BCE) at the northern foot of the Lishan Mountain in the Shaanxi Province with a terracotta army consisting of over 8000 soldiers with accompanying chariots and horses to protect him in the afterlife (UNESCO World Heritage Site 1987).

During the Old and Middle Kingdoms of Ancient Egypt, statues and paintings were often a substitute for human beings, providing archaeologists with a unique depiction of everyday life in the land of the Pharaohs. Egyptian pyramids, of course, were royal funerary structures. Built over a period of 2700 years, they contained the grave proper; an adjacent mortuary temple where priests performed rituals offering food and supplication to the pharaoh's protective spirit; and a valley temple or pavilion, which was often connected by canal to the Nile River. Scores of pyramids dotted the Egyptian landscape, though few survive today having been reduced to ruins and their royal funerary objects long plundered.

When Mausolus, the ruler of Caria (part of ancient Anatolia) died, his widow constructed a large, sepulchral monument to house his remains sometime around 353–350 CE in what today is modern Turkey. Considered one of the Seven Wonders of the Ancient World (Kostof 1995, 9), the term "Mausoleum" was spawned. The most iconic mausoleum ever constructed has to be the Taj Mahal at Agra, India. Built in 1631 CE of fine-grained white marble by the Mughal emperor Shah Jahan for his favorite wife, Mumtaz Mahal – truly a Wonder of the Modern World.

We re-entered the Pitkin Tomb on 24 August 2000, accompanied by Dr Albert B. Harper, director of the Henry C. Lee Institute of Forensic Sciences at the University of New Haven and his students, volunteers from the Friends of the Office of State Archaeology, Inc. (FOSA) led by David G. Cooke, an amateur archaeologist from Rocky Hill, Connecticut, the Friends of Center Cemetery, members of the Connecticut Gravestone Network and Town of East Hartford Public Works personnel who opened the metal door allowing our investigation and identification of the human remains unexpectedly found reposing inside.

We were introduced to Center Cemetery archivist, John J. Spaulding who, armed with a copy of A.P. Pitkin's *Pitkin Family in America* (1887), acquainted us with page lxvii referencing a list of 18 members of the Pitkin family who had been originally placed in the vault with their names, ages and dates of death tabulated. Although the record indicated that all 18 had been removed, John could only confirm five interments outside the tomb. Hence, John's research estimated that 13 individuals might still repose in the structure's chamber.

Town workers installed generator-powered floodlights, so Dave Cooke and I entered the tomb carefully negotiating four brownstone steps down to the subterranean earthen floor. Constructed from the ground level were two 18-inch (ca. 46 cm) high brick partitions lining both sides of the center aisle front-to-back with perpendicular rows of bricks separated every 2 ft (ca. 60 cm) extending to the side and rearmost walls of the tomb which supported coffins and kept them from contact with the loam floor (Fig. 2.7). This architectural form created 11 compartments that the coffins balanced over. Unfortunately, desiccating atrophy of the wooden boxes collapsed human remains and fragmented coffin material, filling the compartments with commingled bones, wood and hardware.

Observing the disarray of mortuary materials and skeletal remains, someone suggested that the tomb had been vandalized. My response was that the tomb had not been disturbed, but the observed "disarray" was the natural result of progressive deterioration and collapse of wooden coffins stacked on top of one another.

The majority of the coffins were lined along the sidewalls in two rows toward the center aisle. Along with wooden coffins, there were three metal caskets, including Dr Edward Pitkin's Fisk Metallic Case, whose name interestingly enough does not appear in the family genealogy as residing in the tomb. Another coffin plate identified Clarissa, Dr Pitkin's unmarried daughter, whose casket was placed on planks bridging the two center rows of bricks of the main aisle (Fig. 2.8). We assumed, due to her position in the tomb, that she was the last burial, laid to rest in 1888. Between them was the third metal casket having no nameplate but which we hypothesized accommodated the mortal remains of Clarissa Roberts Pitkin, the doctor's wife and their daughter's namesake, which subsequent forensic investigation verified. A quick count of the coffins and associated skeletal remains concluded that the tomb contained 16 individuals. John Spaulding was correct – 13 burials anticipated from the Pitkin genealogy (Pitkin 1887) and three additional

Fig. 2.7. Interior of Pitkin Tomb, showing coffins balanced on brick partitions (Photo: John J. Spaulding).

burials interred from Dr Edward Pitkin's nuclear family, which were unrecorded in genealogical or cemetery records.

The first order of business was mapping the internal structure of the tomb and the positions of all coffins and skeletal remains, many of which were comingled into the compartments between the brick partitions. Once organized and numbered, the spatial location of burials would be used as part of the identification process. The coffins were placed lengthwise north-to-south with heads oriented north toward the tomb's entrance. The deceased was carried feet first down the steps and placed in positions on top the bricks, or upon previously laid coffins, parallel to the sidewalls of the tomb. Burial #10 was the lone exception, located against the far southern wall, oriented west to east with the head to the west. This singular individual alone along the back wall was forensically confirmed as the family patriarch and builder of the tomb, Squire Elisha Pitkin.

Once numbered, we selected a single burial at a time for forensic examination, recording estimations of age, sex, dental health, pathology and stature to each individual for comparison with the list compiled in the family genealogy. Diagnostic skeletal elements were removed from each burial and handed out to Dr Harper, including the cranium, pelvis, and a single lower extremity long bone, typically the femur. Since the Town of East Hartford preferred not to leave the tomb open due to fears of

1876
BURIAL CHRONOLOGY • PITKIN TOMB
Center Cemetery, East Hartford, CT

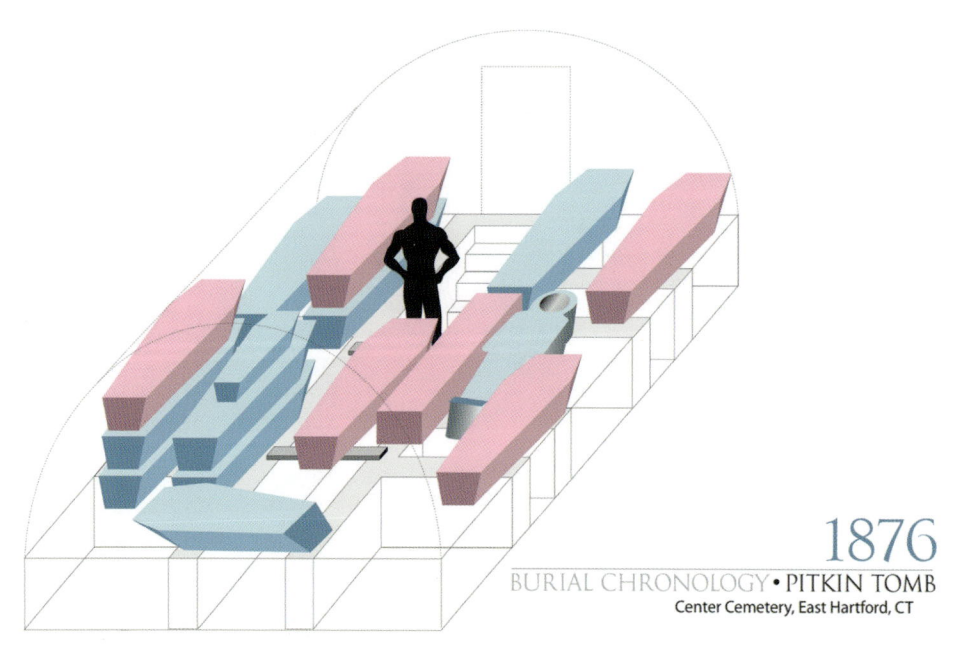

Fig. 2.8. Schematic showing positions of the coffins, interior, Pitkin Family Tomb, Center Cemetery, East Hartford, Connecticut (Credit: Connecticut State Museum of Natural History, University of Connecticut). Blue = "male" coffins and pink = "female" coffins.

vandalism, they requested we complete our task within a single working day, thus a more thorough forensic laboratory analysis of each skeletal element was not achievable. Nonetheless, our on-site laboratory was successful in extracting information needed for identification, which was the main goal of our inquiry, and the skeletal elements selected provided our best means of accomplishing that objective as expeditiously as possible.

I continued the interior mapping of the tomb and the marshaling of skeletal elements to the outdoor laboratory where Al Harper and his students examined the bones. Upon completion of the forensic evaluation, all skeletal remains were returned as close as possible to their original location in the vault.

With Clarissa, Jr's casket bridging the center aisle, movement around the tomb was restricted. In order to access all four corners of the chamber we had to balance on the brick partitions, careful not to damage any skeletal elements strewn along the earthen floor. Dividing the interior of the tomb into sections, I worked one area at a time, recording individual burials and mapping their locations. Amazingly, a couple of the stacked coffins had maintained their positions even though sideboards had popped with the wood's desiccation. Where the bottom boards remained intact, the skeletons were still articulated in a supine position, hands crossed over the chest or pelvic area.

One of my concerns reviewing John Spaulding's archival data was the closeness in age and sex among deceased members of the family, especially since we could not transport any skeletal elements to the university laboratory for more detailed analysis. For example, three of Elisha and Hannah's sons, Solomon (aged 26), Horace (aged 19) and Stephen (aged 30) died within ten years in age of each other, making it more difficult to distinguish in the analysis of fully adult skeletons. In addition, Elisha's grandson and namesake died in 1821 at the age of 22. Thus, distinguishing these four young adult males from the forensic evidence at hand could be challenging, especially with varying degrees of organic preservation and deviations in cranial suture closures and bone fusion rates (which are age related), so a subdivision of the identification process focused on the spatial location of each burial and the degree of coffin stacking.

We made the assumption that coffins lying directly on the bricks represent earlier interments while those superimposed above came later in chronological order. So, understanding the stratigraphic position of coffins throughout the tomb and the known date of death of each candidate assisted in separating out individuals which Dr Harper and his team could then identify, say, as "young adult male." In addition, funerary hardware such as nails, handles, and hinges were recorded as material means of understanding chronology through evolving mortuary technology into the early 19th century. The archaeological mapping and stratigraphy inside the tomb and Dr Harper's forensic efforts outside the tomb combined our efforts of achieving the goal of identifying specific family members.

The overall dental health of the Pitkin family interred in the tomb was poor and typical of the time period. The skeletal evidence exhibited a high percentage of abscessed teeth (33%) and caries (25%). Every individual, including young adults, had some tooth loss due to periodontal disease, while three older adults were completely edentulous (see glossary for explanation of technical terms). There was no evidence of fillings or appliances that would have suggested the family had access to a dental professional despite their prosperity (Bellantoni 2000).

Every older adult presented signs of osteoarthritis, most severe in the leg and hip joints. Clarissa, Dr Pitkin's wife, exhibited friable bone loss due to osteoporosis. Length measurements for the femur (thigh bone) from five males yielded an estimated average stature of 5 ft 7 in (170 cm) and 5 ft 2 in (157 cm) from six female specimens. For a relatively prominent and well-to-do family, they exhibited many of the same health problems as the majority of their New England contemporaries during the late 18th and early 19th centuries.

Combining forensic data derived from 15 skeletal remains (Dr Edward Pitkin remained inside the Fisk Burial Case), archaeological data based on spatial location of the remains, and the family genealogy of recorded individuals interred in the tomb, we were able to provide positive identifications for the following people:

> *Squire Elisha Pitkin (1733-1819); his wife, Hannah (1740-1811); his sons, Elisha (1758-1802), Timothy (1762-1815), Dr. Edward (1769-1851); his grandson, Roswell, Jr (1802-1815); Timothy's wife, Jerusha (1762-1819); and Edward's wife and daughter, Clarissa Roberts (1783-1864) and Clarissa (1824-1876).*

Less positive identifications were made for the following individuals due to their similarity in sex and age at death:

> Squire Pitkin's sons, Solomon (1767-1793), Horace (1782-1801), Stephen (1787-1817) and Roswell (1775-1808); two wives of Roswell Pitkin: Electa Kimball (1780-1806) and Mary Cheney (1779-1813); and Squire's grandson, Elisha (1799-1821).

Not all of Squire Elisha Pitkin's children were buried in his family tomb. The grave of his daughter, **Elizabeth** (1764–1821), is unknown and his youngest daughter **Hannah** (1778–1781) is interred at Center Cemetery across Main Drive in proximity to other Pitkin families. All of the Squire's offspring that were originally interred and then removed from the tomb were from his son Samuel's (1760–1839) family, including **Samuel**; his wife, **Sarah** (1764–1843); their son, **Samuel L.** (1803–1845); and the daughter of Samuel L., **Sarah Ann** (1833–1835). Together they are interred in Center Cemetery south of Hill Drive about 200 ft (ca. 60 m) to the east near their 10 ft/3 m long granite sarcophagus.

We could find no extant records as to when Elisha Pitkin constructed his family's tomb. The earliest burial inside the tomb was **Solomon**, who died in 1793; yet his sister, Hannah, who died four years earlier was interred in another portion of the cemetery. So, we contend that the tomb was probably built sometime between 1790 and 1793. In 1793, Squire Pitkin turned 60 years of age and his thoughts may have turned to providing for his final resting place even though he would outlive almost his entire family (Spaulding 2001).

****

On 3 September 2001 over two dozen Pitkin descendants, some coming from as far away as the United Kingdom, gathered at the face of the Pitkin Tomb at Center Cemetery for a family reunion and to dedicate a 5 × 5 ft (1.5 × 1.5 m) granite marker displaying the names of the 16 Pitkin ancestors lying therein. East Hartford Mayor Timothy D. Larson proclaimed the date "Pitkin Day" in honor of one of the most prominent families to settle on the east side of the "Great River" and whose ancestors served the town as soldiers, various public committee members, mill owners, Justices of the Peace, selectmen, civic judges, ferry keepers, surveyors, manufacturers, and, of course, as the last Governor of the Connecticut Colony. A wonderful heritage brought back to memory owing to the occupants of an "empty" tomb!

Fig. 2.9. Memorial Stone Placed by the Friends of Center Cemetery, Inc. listing 16 of Elisha Pitkin's family interred within the tomb, East Hartford, Connecticut (Photo: John J. Spaulding).

Chapter 3

The Tomb of Gershom Bulkeley and His Descendants

*Once more detained him there;
And, stirred by hauntings, he must needs repair
To where the tomb was. Lo, it stood still wasting
In no man's care.*

Thomas Hardy, *The Obliterate Tomb*

Halloween has always been a celebrated night for tomfoolery. However, in 1933, four high school students attending Bacon Academy, Colchester, Connecticut, may have taken mischief-making a bit too far when they broke into a timeworn tomb in the town's ancient burial ground. What merriment if they could detach an actual human skull from its corpse and frighten fellow costumed mates! The centuries-old wooden door of the tomb would have shattered easily for them to enter and the interior was littered with many decomposed skeletons, so stealing a skull for pranking on this ominous night was an effortless affair. Placing a readily available skull on a pole, they hoisted the cranium high and paraded around the Town Green, obviously creating a huge commotion.

So much so that the town elders were summoned to investigate the uproar. And when they did, no one was more distraught than the minister of Colchester's First Congregational Church since it was *his* son who was leading the procession and carrying the staff bearing the skull! The minister was deeply humiliated and ordered the boys, including his son, to be severely reprimanded (meaning a good beating), and the skull immediately returned to the ancient tomb.

Due to the disruption of the community, the town's leaders decided to close up the old tomb for good to prevent any further desecration by pranking teenagers in the future. The next day, the four chastised students were commanded by the school's principal to seal up the tomb once and for all. They were instructed to bury the mausoleum under loads of soil brought in by truck, completely eradicating any visible sign of the structure; they removed the desiccated wooden gate and replaced it with brick and mortar, sealing up the doorway; they then uprooted standing footstones

Fig. 3.1. Rediscovered marble tablets identifying the "Tomb of Gershom Bulkeley and his Descendants", Colchester Burial Ground, Colchester, Connecticut (Photo: John J. Spaulding).

and small tombstones from graves throughout the aged cemetery and stacked them facedown filling the entire stairwell descending to the tomb's below-ground entrance (Church 2005, 1). The tomb was made impenetrable, vanishing from sight except as an inconspicuous mound of earth on the sloping west side of the cemetery. In fact, they did such a good job in obliterating the tomb (apologies to Thomas Hardy) that within three generations there was no cultural memory in town that the tomb ever existed!

The old burying ground eventually lapsed into disrepair and the small knoll at its western end sat unnoticed and overlooked. Even the cemetery's restoration in 1991 paid no attention to the unremarkable protuberance on the hill. It was not until the spring of 2002, when town workers were clearing a tree line of dense vegetation to erect period fencing around the cemetery's border that folks started to pay attention to the obscure earthen embankment. And that was because the workers unexpectedly found three broken pieces of a large marble tablet downslope from the mound (Fig. 3.1) which, when placed together, read:

The Tomb of Gershom Bulkeley and his Descendants.

****

As Dave Cooke and I returned to his home after a day conducting rescue archaeological excavations at an 18th-century colonial house site slated for demolition, his wife, June, greeted us at the back door saying that Arthur Liverant, an antique dealer in Colchester, Connecticut and a friend of Dave's, was on the phone and wanted to speak with me. Arthur related the story of the newly uncovered marble fragments at the Colchester Burial Ground. The Bulkeleys were actively involved with the cemetery's current restoration, he said, and they were very excited to learn more about the rediscovered tomb. In fact, the family was already developing plans to rebuild the crypt. However, they had no genealogical, church or town records indicating which of their ancestors might be buried within and they felt it essential to know this as part of the restoration project. Arthur was aware of our involvement with the Squire Elisha Pitkin Tomb (see Chapter 2) and the identifications we were able to make of Pitkin ancestors, and inquired if we could conduct a similar forensic analysis of anticipated skeletal remains inside the Gershom Bulkeley Tomb. Believing that we might be able to assist, we set up a meeting at the cemetery with the Bulkeley family and town officials. Developing a research team, I immediately contacted John Spaulding to commence genealogical investigation into the history of the Bulkeley family of Colchester (Spaulding 2006) as he had undertaken with the Pitkin family of East Hartford, and Roger Thompson, a retired insurance executive, began land deed research into Bulkeley holdings in Colchester.

The Colchester Burial Ground lies behind the Federated Church and former Bacon Academy at the junction of Main Street (Route 85) and Linwood Avenue (Route 16). Proceeding east from the latter thoroughfare, turn right onto a split driveway, bear left up the hill toward the back of the church and the old graveyard is immediately on the right with an identifying stone plaque at the entrance. Continue along the lower slope and you pass an open area with no stone markers that we suspect contains the graves of the town's African captives, including those owned by the Bulkeley family. The stone and brick tomb rises straight ahead facing west. The Bulkeley Family Tomb remains the sole above-ground chamber in the cemetery. The only sandstone tablet in the burying ground belongs to the Rev. John Bulkeley with its inset heraldic slate with a helmeted knight and three bulls closer to the church he preached in (Slater 1987, 143).

Meeting onsite (30 May 2002) with John, Dave and myself, were First Selectwoman Jenny Contois; Colchester Municipal Historian and Town Public Works director Stanley Moroch, who originally discovered the marble slabs; Arthur Liverant; and Peter Bulkeley, a lineal descendant and president of the Gardner-Bulkeley Cemetery Association, Inc. Stanley reviewed the discovery of the tombstone slabs and what was known about the tomb's history (which was very little). Peter Bulkeley discussed his family's plan to renovate the burial chamber to its original 18th-century appearance and, since they could find no burial records, requested that we enter the tomb and conduct forensic examinations with the goal of identifying his ancestors. The Town of Colchester owns the burying ground and as such Jenny gave her blessings and support to the project. We walked over the area, examined the small mound (Fig. 3.2) and I thought to myself that this should be doable. From the outside, the buried vault looked much smaller than the Pitkin Tomb, so I imagined there were probably fewer than ten people interred within. It would not be the first time I was wrong (or, I suppose, the last).

Fig. 3.2. The earthen mound overlying the concealed Gershom Bulkeley Tomb partially uncovered (Photo: John J. Spaulding).

****

The surname has been spelled Bulkey, Buckley, Buikileh, Buckly, and Bulkley, but the Rev. Peter (1583–1659), the first of the lineage to journey to New England in 1635, wrote it as "Bulkeley" (Chapman 1875, 18) and the family has adamantly maintained that particular spelling to the present day.

The Reverend Peter Bulkeley was descended from a long line of barons and nobles in England (Jacobus 1933). The motto of the family coat of arms, *Nec temere, nee timide* ("Neither Rashly nor Timidly") resonates with descendants to this very day. Peter's father, Edward, was a noted minister in the Church of England and trained his son to follow in his footsteps. Born in Odell, Bedfordshire, England on 31 January 1583, young Peter attended St John's College at Cambridge at the tender age of 16, where he would receive a Bachelor of Divinity degree, returning to preach the Gospel in his home town, succeeding his father in that role for the next 20 years. Both father and son were independent thinkers and by the early 1630s, Peter's sermons had become increasingly opposed to the requirements of the Anglican Church as his sentiments gravitated toward the Puritan movement (Jacobus 1933, 100). When parishioners complained to Church authorities, Peter was defrocked of his ministry (Jacobus 1933, 93). Recognizing that it was in his best interest to remove himself from England, he absconded to New England to associate with his fellow Puritans relocating in the New World colonies.

Rev. Peter Bulkelely arrived in Cambridge, Massachusetts, by mid-decade as a component of the Great Puritan Migration, bringing with him some of the family's assets and joining the church in Boston (Jacobus 1933, 101). Before long, he established himself as a leading member of the community respected for his staunch Puritan behavior and beliefs, and convincing a number of admiring families to uproot and follow him "into the woods and settle on the plantation at Musketaquid", where they founded the Town of Concord (Jacobus 1933, 104). Rev. Bulkeley led a full life of obedience and benevolence towards his parishioners, practically giving away his entire fortune to those in need. He served on a number of synods and had several sermons published. Nevertheless, working in the "wilderness" of Concord left him inconspicuous and under-appreciated among his peers when compared to the ministers of Boston who, to this day, receive greater acclaim.

Rev. Peter died on 9 March 1659 in Cambridge, but not before leaving a considerable pedigree. He had 12 children (ten sons and two daughters) with his first wife, Jane Allen, all of whom were born in England. After eight years a widower, he remarried to Grace Chetwood and had four more children, including Gershom, the eldest and first of the Bulkeley family born in New England (6 December 1636). Grace would survive Peter traveling with her son, Gershom, to New London, Connecticut, and dying there on 21 April 1663 (Chapman 1875).

Gershom Bulkeley was an eclectic force to be reckoned with and one of the exceptional personalities of 17th-century New England. He graduated from Harvard College in 1655 where he met and married Sarah Chauncy, daughter of Harvard President Charles Chauncy (see Chapter 5). Gershom left Concord to become the second minister of the Congregational Church in New London in 1661, serving that parish for 6 years before "uneasiness" in the community lead him to relocate to Wethersfield on the Connecticut River in 1667. There, Gershom became the second pastor of the church and began to devote his attention to the practice of medicine and surgery. When King Philip's War broke out in 1675, Gershom was appointed as surgeon to the army fighting to put down the Native American rebellion spreading throughout New England. He was wounded in the thigh when his regiment was attacked near Wachuset Hill in Massachusetts (Jacobus 1933, 117).

Recovering from his injury, he would go on to study chemistry, philosophy, and alchemy, while developing skills in surveying and the operation of a grist mill, mastering several languages including Greek, Latin and Dutch, serving as a magistrate for the Colonial Government and being commissioned Justice of the Peace. Concerned that the authority of the Connecticut's upper leadership was eroding the democratic principles he espoused, Gershom wrote a series of blistering pamphlets against autocratic rule. He was also a conundrum, in that while usually depicted as "an eccentric, a gadfly, a malcontent or worse," Gershom was in every sense a strict royalist, a Tory, whose loyalty to the Crown was unquestioned, yet the science he espoused would, ironically, lead to new political and social realities in the next century that would contribute to the upcoming American rebellion against the English monarchy he was faithful to (Jodziewicz 1988, 38–9).

Most notably, Gershom was one of the few Puritan voices skeptical about evidence presented in the New England Witch Trials against those accused, especially in the case of Mercy Holbridge Disbrow. Gershom was largely responsible for Mary's reprieve after she was convicted of witchcraft in Fairfield, Connecticut, in 1696 (Jacobus 1933, 126). Earlier, in the 1669 witchcraft case of Katherine Harrison of Wethersfield, Gershom Bulkeley and Jonathan Winthrop, Jr, worked together to undermine "the legal foundations for convicting witches in Connecticut and removed intellectual study of the occult from ministerial suspicion and official scrutiny" (Woodward 2010, 212). This case in particular had a profound effect on the response of the church and colonial government officials in pursuing witchcraft allegations in New England. Gershom Bulkeley was an erudite, outspoken Renaissance man, widely revered and, yet, reviled for he never worried about speaking his mind to whomever and whenever or to any subject.

Gershom and Sarah Chauncy Bulkeley had six children, including a son christened John, born in Wethersfield on 9 June 1679. John Bulkeley married Sarah Prentice in 1701 and sired 12 children. He graduated from Harvard College receiving a Degree in Divinity (the fifth consecutive generation of Protestant ministers in the family) and was ordained as the first pastor of the First Church of Colchester, Connecticut, where the couple moved to in 1703, and where his descendants would reside and be buried for generations to come.

When, in 1724, a debate arose about the rights of Native Americans to receive compensation for their lands, Rev. John Bulkeley wrote a thesis developing the argument that since the Indian did not "improve" the land in the European sense of "changing nature," that is, they did not adhere to Biblical rights of "dominium" over land, animals and plants and, since they had been "subdued" by British Puritanism, they, thus, had no rights to occupy their own land and the English had no responsibilities to compensate Indigenous Peoples for the taking their territory (Bulkeley 1725; Poteet 1975, 232; Cronon 1983, 53). A Euro-centric argument if ever there was one.

The Reverend Nathaniel Chauncey, son of the Harvard President and John's maternal uncle, penned of the Bulkeley family of that time: "Mr. Gershom Bulkeley, father of John, I have heard mentioned as a truly great man and eminent in his skill in chemistry, and the father of Gershom, and grandfather of John, Peter Bulkeley of Concord, was esteemed in his day as one of the greatest men in this part of the world. But, by all that I have been able to collect, the Colchester Bulkeley (John) surpassed his predecessors in the strength of his intellectual power" (Chapman 1875, 91; Jacobus 1933, 139). Reverend John Bulkeley would serve the Colchester congregation for the rest of his life and be honored as one of the highest-ranking clergymen of his time. He passed on 10 June 1731 at 52 years of age. The slate epitaph on the sandstone table over his burial reads:

> *Distinguished for rare ability, extensive learning, the exemplification of many virtues, and the large influence which he exerted for good.*

Of John and Patience's 12 children, the fifth was Gershom (the builder of our tomb), namesake of his celebrated grandfather, born on 4 February 1708/09. Unlike many of his eminent ancestors, Gershom was not a minister or a man of letters, so we know little about his personal life other than what remains available in public records. This we do know: He was a farmer by occupation; married Abigail Robbins sometime in late November 1733 and together they raised eight children (five sons and three daughters); he served with distinction in the colonial militia where he quickly climbed in rank being commissioned Ensign of the North Company of Colchester in 1749, promoted to Lieutenant the following year, and then Captain in May 1752; and he was elected to the Connecticut General Assembly in 1756, serving 2 years as Deputy for Colchester. When the French and Indian War erupted, Captain Gershom Bulkeley and his Colchester Company were mobilized and directed to New York when Fort William Henry on the southern shore of Lake George fell to the enemy in 1757 (Jacobus 1933, 173).

The Rev. John Bulkeley's Last Will and Testament (Chapman 1875, 93) established that Gershom inherited from his father "all the land in ye lane on which he has erected his house with the mill" (Chapman 1875, 93). Gershom was very successful in agribusiness enabling him to hold in hand sufficient financial resources to purchase additional land from his neighbors, piecing together over time one of the largest farms in the region. His growing wealth enticed people in Colchester needing assistance to petition Gershom in lending them cash to pay their taxes, we assume with goodly interest. His landholdings in the western portion of Colchester were extensive, and to labor the expanding farm, he purchased African captives and their offsprings: Jack, Flora, Caesar, Peg and her sons, Jack and Prince. The latter two would be retained by Gershom's descendants and, we assume, were buried in unmarked graves at the Colchester Burial Ground (Jacobus 1933, 173). Similar to Squire Elisha Pitkin, Gershom Bulkeley never manumitted his captives, instead passing them to his heirs.

As his 80th birthday approached, Gershom Bulkeley made the decision to construct a stone and brick mortared tomb for himself and his growing family into the hill of the cemetery behind the First Church where his father and other family members had previously been buried. Gershom was born, bred, worked, worshipped and died (6 May 1788) in Colchester. He was buried in his newly erected family tomb, as would be many of his siblings, his children and their children, and their children's children.

****

Volunteers labored intensely, digging out by hand the earthen embankment, slowly revealing the brick and granite façade of the Bulkeley Tomb. Seven men, armed with hand shovels and picks, toiled at the hidden tomb, while others wheel-barrowed displaced dirt to the back slope of the cemetery, filling a natural depression. Workers soon uncovered the granite steps leading to the below-ground entrance, and piece by piece they cleared the footstones and headstones that had been laid there by the mischievous students in 1933, placing them individually on the open lawn of the cemetery to be later replanted upright at their appropriate gravesites throughout the cemetery. All that remained was the bricked-up wall separating us from the interior of the tomb.

Carefully tapping the grout between the bricks, we were able to remove the top two rows exposing the granite lintel over the doorway providing our first glimpse inside the tomb. Dave Cooke and I stood on the stone steps and leaned forward towards the entrance with a generator-powered light in hand peering through the crevice into the tomb's interior. Agape, I surveyed the inner sanctum, speechless. Unable to stand the suspense, someone behind me inquired anxiously, "Can you see anything?" I couldn't resist responding, "Yes, wonderful things!"

Though obviously appropriating the line from Howard Carter when he first gazed with amazement into the interior of Tutankhamen's Tomb, I actually did not see "wonderful things" within the Bulkeley Tomb. Instead, I beheld collapsed wooden coffins, some top boards still intact and scattered human skeletons spewed about the tomb. The natural collapse of coffins stacked upon each other, some four high and in two parallel rows extending from the center aisle to the side and back walls, resulted in the entire floor being littered with funerary materials. I realized I had been wrong: the Bulkeley Tomb contained twice the number of burials as the Pitkin Tomb amid more disarray (Fig. 3.3). At that moment, the magnitude and logistics of the project appeared daunting.

Fig. 3.3. First view inside the Gershom Bulkeley Tomb (Photo: John J. Spaulding).

The Bulkeley Tomb is an underground "mound" structure with a double-brick arched dome sitting on a cut-granite foundation. The interior bricks were whitewashed with a lime and sand stucco and the coffins were balanced on 10 in (25.4 cm) high brick partitions – two rows running down the center aisle and perpendicular rows extending to the side and back walls every 2 ft/80 cm creating 19 compartments or cells which in between were filled with additional collapsed coffin debris and skeletal remains. The tomb measures 14 ft (4.26 m) in length, 12 ft (3.65 m) in width and 15 ft (4.57 m) high to the center of the arched ceiling. All this was very reminiscent, in size and configuration, to the Pitkin Tomb with the exception that the stone stairs leading into the interior were on the outside of the structure, not inside as at Center Cemetery and that the Bulkeley Tomb housed twice the number of burials.

From the outset it was clear that some of the contents inside the tomb had been rearranged. Not through vandalism, I suspect, but by attempts at reorganizing the tomb's substances, probably in the later 19th century, long after the last of the burials was interred. In the south-west (front right) corner were a number of stacked lids that had been removed from their original coffins, probably after the sideboards began to deteriorate and skeletal remains had collapsed. These coffin lids were elaborate for the time period with brass tacks hammered onto them arranged into initials, age and/or date of death, all proving essential in identifying interred family members. Many lids had heart-motifs, a sign of Christian endearment, surrounding the deceased's life and death statistics. One wooden and three metal nameplates were also recovered. Together, the lids and nameplates furnished a timeframe from 1775 to the mid-1830s with the coffins representing state-of-the-art mortuary furniture at the end of the 18th and into the 19th centuries, a reflection of Gershom Bulkeley's affluence. This time span precedes the widespread use of metal coffins, hence all of the coffins are of various hard and softwood species.

Our initial procedure was to map the interior of the tomb and photo-document each section, allowing us to determine the collapse pattern onto the center aisle, set up a grid to record spatial context and to develop a method of numbering and removal of coffin and human skeletal remains systematically. It was also important to create space for us to maneuver on the brick platforms and the center aisle in order to penetrate the posterior of the tomb, thereby permitting access without disturbing any remains closer to the entrance.

Organizational aspects of the project were more complicated compared to our earlier tomb efforts but fortunately we had an extraordinary team of supporters, including volunteers from the Connecticut Gravestone Network, Friends of the Office of State Archaeology, Colchester Historical Society and the Town of Colchester, who combined contributed over 1200 hours of work at the site. Stanley Moroch saw to our every mechanical and material need; Dave Cooke supervised the volunteer field crews, organizing work details and divisions of labor; John Spaulding served as our official photographer, snapping over 1000 images (Bellantoni and Spaulding 2002); Peter Bulkeley and Susan Bulkeley Daly, family descendants, were onsite most days and compiled an outsized spreadsheet of the family's genealogy that was posted on an easel for convenient reference; and students from four area colleges (University of Connecticut, Boston University, University of New Haven, and Wesleyan University) assisted in note taking, illustration and inventory production.

Once I was able to move about the tomb, I began by numbering every visible coffin with associated human remains and designated alphabetic coding for each partition where disarticulated bones had collapsed (Fig. 3.4). We also formulated a plan for making forensic identifications and obtaining wood and metal samples from each of the coffins. These would facilitate preliminary identifications, which were created

Fig. 3.4. Collapsed coffins with human remains balanced on bottom boards (Photo: John J. Spaulding).

Fig. 3.5. Drs Albert Harper and State Medical Examiner H. Wayne Carver at the Bulkeley Tomb, Colchester, Connecticut (Photo: John J. Spaulding).

Fig. 3.6. University of Connecticut graduate student Kristen Bastis at work with Dr Albert Harper sorting through skeletal remains recovered from the Bulkeley Tomb, Colchester, Connecticut (Photo: John J. Spaulding)

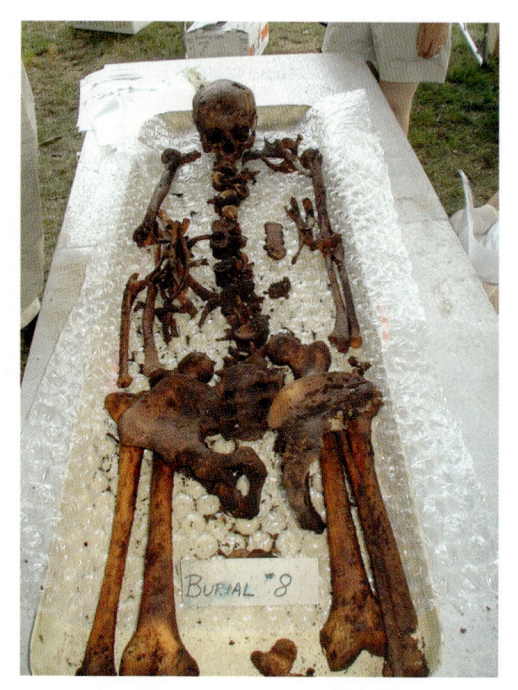

Fig. 3.7. Skeletal remains of Charles Taintor removed from the Bulkeley Tomb for forensic identification (Photo: John J. Spaulding).

both within and outside the tomb, and would eventually accommodate more detailed skeletal and funeral data compiled in the laboratories.

On 2 July 2002 the first burials were ready for removal and on hand to assist were Dr Albert B. Harper, Director of the Henry C. Lee Institute of Forensic Sciences at the University of New Haven, and Dr H. Wayne Carver II, Connecticut State's Chief Medical Examiner (Fig. 3.5). As he did at the Pitkin Tomb, Al Harper stayed on to work with the students, especially training Kristen Bastis (Fig. 3.6), who would write her anthropology Master's thesis at the University of Connecticut on the paleopathology of the Bulkeley Tomb skeletons, recording and identifying preliminary forensic aspects of each individual as they emerged from the crypt (Bastis 2006).

Working with one assistant at a time inside the tomb, I "excavated," recorded and handled each burial separately, working the stacked coffins from top-to-bottom, row-by-row beginning along the center aisle before moving to adjacent rows aligned along the walls. Where unfinished bottom coffin boards with skeletal remains still balancing on them were intact and preserved enough for us to lift without damage, we transferred the complete assemblage, supported by plywood planks, out of the tomb. There students and volunteers recorded, cleaned and sorted human remains, wood, and metal, enfolded them in bubble wrap, and packaged the labeled bags into containers for transport to our laboratories at the University of Connecticut. Skeletons not resting on bottom boards were placed on long rectangular trays as anatomically correctly as possible, and carefully extricated from the tomb (Fig. 3.7).

Similarly, we excavated the south-west corner of the tomb by removing each of the stacked coffin lids separately buttressed on plywood. While the forensic analysis of the individual skeletal remains would take time, the brass tack patterns on the coffin lids were an early key to the identification of Bulkeley family members interred in the tomb. Every coffin had patterned lids or nameplates, though two lids had deteriorated to the point that the only surviving features were the numbers "67" and "70", most likely referring to ages at death, but with no corresponding initials that could be reassembled to establish family identities.

The Bulkeley genealogy (Chapman 1875; Jacobus 1933) provided essential vital statistics for each family member back to the Reverend Peter Bulkeley, enabling immediate determination of Gershom's descendants represented in the tomb. In addition, John Spaulding researched the locations of known "Bulkeley" tombstones recorded in other area cemeteries, even finding four generations of descendants buried as far away as Moretown, Vermont (Spaulding 2006). Hence, by eliminating family interred elsewhere and focusing on those whose coffin lids were within the tomb (Figs 3.8 and 3.9), this initial field research helped establish potential family candidates and provided a baseline for the forensic identifications.

While the majority of all the coffin lids were stacked in the south-west corner separate from their corresponding burials, one coffin lid reclined directly on top of the skeletal remains of Rhoda (Jones) Kellogg Bulkeley (1750–1807), who died at 56 years of age in 1807 (Fig. 3.10). Rhoda was Gershom's childless daughter-in-law, the third wife of his son, Roger, who also resides in the tomb. Eventual forensic analysis of Rhoda's skeletal remains corroborated her lid's inscription.

Fig. 3.8. Coffin lid of Gershom's brother, Peter Bulkeley (1712–1798) (Photo: John J. Spaulding).

Fig. 3.9. Coffin lid of Gershom's son, John Bulkley (1738–1807) (Photo: John J. Spaulding).

Fig. 3.10. Coffin lid and skeletal remains of Rhoda Jones Kellogg Bulkeley (1750–1807) (Photo: John J. Spaulding).

While some of the Bulkeley family coffin lids were badly deteriorated and required reassembling in order to read their full inscriptions, the majority were sufficiently preserved to permit immediate genealogical identifications (Table 3.1). Since many of the lids were stacked away from the burials they had been displaced from, matching the biological remains to coffin lid information was essential in demonstrating which descendants were actually in the tomb and had not been removed in the past to another cemetery location. Of the 33 lids recovered, forensic analyses confirmed the identities of 29 Bulkeley family out of 31 skeletal remains still sheltered in the tomb. Oddly, we never found a coffin lid for Gershom Bulkeley, the tomb's builder!

Consanguineal and affinal relationships to Gershom Bulkeley of individuals in the tomb include his wife, Abigail, four sons, one sister, one brother, one nephew, six grandsons, one granddaughter, four great grandsons, two great granddaughters, five daughters-in-law and one granddaughter-in-law (Spaulding 2006). One nameplate in the tomb identifies a child named "Spencer Jones," but we could find no genealogical information identifying his family relationship.

For 12 working days, we painstakingly removed all associated material from stacked coffins resting on the brick partitions and, once completed, turned our attention to

Table 3.1. Bulkeley coffin lid identifications based on The Bulkeley Genealogy *(Jacobus 1933).*

Date	Name	Information[1]	Decoration
1775	Gershom Taintor	T 20 775 Æ 10	Heart
1788	Charles Taintor?	At 8 Y 27 D 88	No heart tacks on edge
1788	Gershom Bulkeley	At 81 July?	No heart spaced letters
1788	John Bulkeley	JB Æ TAT 29 Oct 8 1788	No heart tacks on edge spaced 13
1788	?	DG? 1788	Initials /age in heart tacks on edge
1793	Abigail R Bulkeley	AB Æ TAT 79 D Sep 12 1793	Initials in heart spaced tacks
1798	Peter Bulkeley	PB Æ TAT 87 March AD 1798	Initials in heart spaced tacks
1798	Sarah B T Wells	Æ TAT 96 1798	No heart, no edge
1801	William Bulkeley	WB Æ 39 1801	Heart and tacks on edge cherry
1801	Judith Worthington	JB Æ 59 1801	Initials in heart and tacks on edge
1804	Asa Bulkeley	AB Æ 30 1804	Heart and tacks on edge
1804	Jershua	JB Æ 4 1804	No heart spaced tacks on edge
1805	Anna Bulkeley	ABR B Feb 14 AD 1802 D Sep 29 1805	No heart spaced letters
1806	John Worthington	IW Æ 33 1806	Heart on cherry
1806?	Sarah B Taintor?	70	No drawing of lid
1807	John Bulkeley	JB Æ 69 1807	Heart and tacks on edge
1807	Rhoda J K Bulkeley	RB Æ 56 1807	Heart and tacks on edge
1808	Harriet Olmstead	HB Æ 22 1808	Heart and tacks on edge
1810	Daniel Bulkeley	DB 66	No lid?
1810	Chauncey Wells	CW Æ 66 1744 1810	Fragment no heart?
1811	George Bulkeley	GB Æ 31 1811	Heart and tacks on edge
1811	Mary C Bulkeley	MB Æ 69 1811	Heart and tacks on edge
1812	Lois D Bulkeley	LB -70 -12	Heart and tacks on edge
1812	David Bulkeley	DB Æ 63 1812	Heart and tacks on edge
1813	Oliver Bulkeley	OB Æ 11	Small heart no tacks on edge
1817	Epaphroditus Bulkeley	EB Æ 25	Heart
1819	Benjamin F Bulkeley	BFB Æ 13	Heart
1819?	Rodger Bulkeley?	67	No lid?
1821	Sarah B Rodgers	SR Æ 40	Heart? Dots fragment
1821	Joshua Bulkeley	JB Æ 81	Heart &?
1826	Richard Bulkeley	RB Æ 2	No heart no edge spaced letters
1826	Hannah B Bulkeley	HB Æ 76	Small heart spaced tacks
1832	Gershom Bulkeley	Gershom Bulkeley 1788- 1832 Age 44	No lid/metal plate

[1]Column lists the numeric and alphabetic arrangement of brass tacks on the lid of each coffin.
Table reconstructed from Bastis (2006, 59)

BULKELEY TOMB
Colchester Burying Ground, Colchester, CT

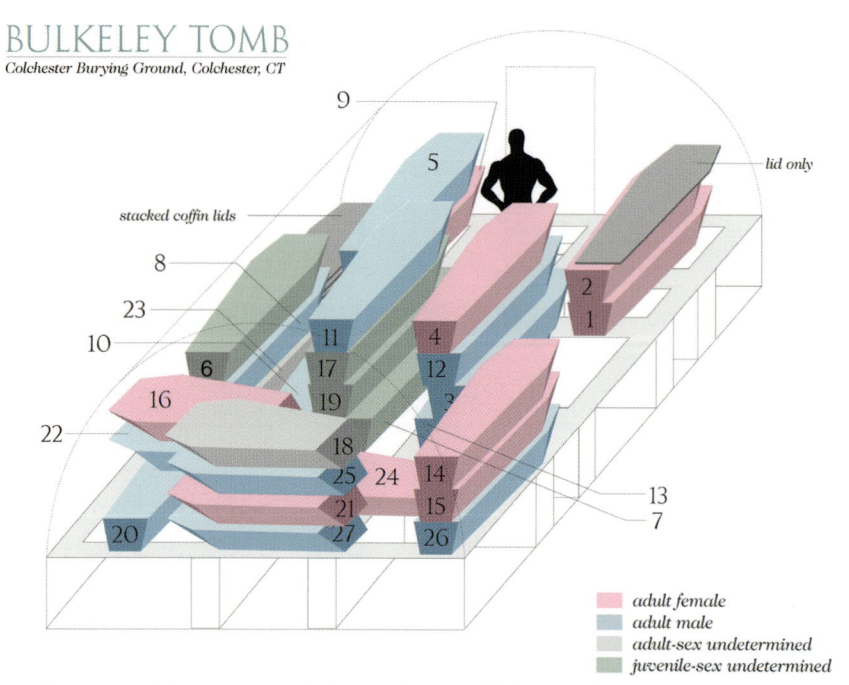

Fig. 3.11. Schematic of the interior of the Gershom Bulkeley Tomb showing their original coffin placements (Credit: Connecticut State Museum of Natural History, University of Connecticut).

the mostly disarticulated remains collapsed between them. Each of these "Units" was given a number designation and excavated and recorded separately. We made no attempts to identify individuals recovered from these units in the field but secured them for future analysis in the laboratory. Eventually, the Bulkeley Tomb was emptied and a schematic of the tomb's interior could be reconstructed (Fig. 3.11). Once these tasks were completed, the structural restoration process began.

****

Gershom Bulkeley's family entombed with him and his wife Abigail left a record of many extraordinary accomplishments. His sister Sarah Bulkeley Trumbull Welles (1702–1798) married Joseph Trumbull when she was 25 years old. Joseph's brother, Jonathan Trumbull served as the "War Governor" of Connecticut during the American Revolution and his cousin John, was a noted Revolutionary Era poet. Unfortunately, Joseph Trumbull would venture to the West Indies on a business trip in December 1731 never to be "seen or heard of" again (Jacobus 1933, 171). Sarah died in Colchester at the age of 96, having lived almost the entire 18th century, and was buried in her brother's newly built family tomb in 1798. Likewise, Gershom's brother Peter (1712–1798), who died the same year as Sarah, was also buried in the tomb after a

3. The Tomb of Gershom Bulkeley and His Descendants

life full of military and political achievement: he was commissioned Captain of the Company in New Salem parish in 1747; Deputy for Colchester to the Connecticut General Assembly for 15 sessions; and Justice of the Peace for Hartford County from 1766–1779 (Jacobus 1933, 175).

Of the patriarch's five sons, three were buried in the tomb: Daniel, who served as Lieutenant of Colchester men under Captain Eliphalet Bulkeley at the Battle of Lexington in 1775; John, who was also commissioned Lieutenant of the Second Co. Twenty-fifth Regiment in 1776; and William, a farmer like his father, who rapidly responded when a special messenger dispatched by Gen. George Washington arrived in Colchester bearing the news of the American Army's distress. William "yoked up his oxen" and trekked south-west toward Philadelphia, transporting some of the first food relief to reach Valley Forge in 1777 (Davino 2003).

The entire Colchester Bulkeley clan was instrumental in providing beef and other provisions to the Continental Army. When General Israel Putnam's regiments, encamped in Redding, Connecticut, during the harsh winter of 1778–79, were suffering from starvation (Cruson 2011), Colchester farmers loaded oxen wagons with supplies and herded beef cattle to help sustain the Patriot Army. Joseph Joslin, Jr writes that "on March 8, they loaded carts with four bundles of pressed hay apiece, and six teams, together with sixty oxen, set out, after waiting at 'old Gershom Bulkeley's (farm)'" (Brown 1976, 44).

Reposed in the tomb also was Gershom's great-grandson, Epaphroditus Bulkeley (1791–1817), who had served as Sergeant during the War of 1812 (Davino 2003). We have no record to support that his war experience may have caused this veteran with the biblical name to perish in his youthful 25th year, but we could find no accounts as to how and why he died. We do know that he had two sophisticated (for their time) dental appliances made for his upper anterior teeth, which he may have lost to trauma (Fig. 3.12). In the tomb associated with his burial, we recovered a pair of upper partials for individual teeth. The two dentures are gold-plated to securely fit the palate with molded porcelain to simulate incisors.

Probably the most notable branch of the Bulkeley family is derived from Gershom's brother John's lineal descendants. John's great grandson, Eliphalet Adams Bulkeley (1803–1872) was born in Colchester and, as did many Bulkeley youths, attended Bacon Academy. Though Eliphalet went on to study law at Yale College, he would receive great recognition in the business industry by founding and becoming the first presidents of both the Connecticut Mutual Life Insurance Company in 1846

Fig. 3.12. Gold and porcelain dental partials from the burial of Epaphroditus Bulkeley (1791-1817) (Photo: John J. Spaulding).

Fig. 3.13. Morgan Gardner Bulkeley (1837-1922) (Credit: New York Public Library Digital Collection).

and the Aetna Life Insurance Company in 1853 (Walsh 2010). Eliphalet's wife was Lydia Smith Morgan Bulkeley, first cousin to New York Governor Edwin Denison Morgan (see Chapter 6) and a distant cousin to financier, J.P. Morgan. Eliphalet moved the family from Colchester to Hartford to be near his business interest where he and his descendants would be buried in the city's Cedar Hill Cemetery.

Eliphalet and Lydia's son, Morgan Gardner Bulkeley (1837–1922) took over the helm of Aetna Life Insurance Co. as its third president and became the 54th Governor of the State of Connecticut, occupying both positions at the same time (Fig. 3.13). This proved fortuitous when the state legislature refused to appropriate money for government operations due to an election deadlock in 1890. Bulkeley had Aetna pay the state's bills until the next election! During that same election stalemate when neither party would recognize a clear winner, the state comptroller decided to change the lock on the Governor's door until the matter could be settled. Bulkeley, indignant at being shut out of his own office, grabbed a crowbar and broke his way in. As a result, he was nicknamed the "Crow-Bar Governor" (Murphy 2010). In 1896, he ran unsuccessfully as a Vice Presidential candidate with running mate, William McKinley, but later won election to the U.S. Senate representing Connecticut in 1905. If all this weren't enough, Morgan G. Bulkeley was chosen as the first president of baseball's National League in 1876. His plaque can be seen at Cooperstown, New York, on the walls of the National Baseball Hall of Fame and Museum, to which he was elected in 1937 in only its second year of balloting.

****

Unlike the Pitkin Tomb project, the Town of Colchester and the Bulkeley family gave permission to remove skeletal remains for laboratory examination. Pathological analysis were conducted by Lenore Barbian and Paul Sledzik of the National Museum of Health and Medicine, Armed Forces Institute of Pathology in Washington, DC, and by Kristen Bastis, anthropology graduate student at the University of Connecticut. Together, they observed a number of interesting patterns involving disease, trauma and evidence of medical treatment. For example, many of the pathological conditions represented are well-healed fractures, various degrees of osteoarthritic development, and other non-infectious degenerative joint diseases, all of which are consistent with what we would expect from agricultural lifestyles of the late 18th and early 19th centuries (Barbian and Sledzik 2005).

Four adult males suffered broken bones: Gershom's son, Daniel Bulkeley (1744–1810) had a broken right clavicle (collar bone); his grandson, William Bulkeley (1761–1801) had two broken left ribs; and his brother, Peter Bulkeley (1712–1798) suffered broken ribs, clavicle and trauma to his atlas (first cervical, neck) vertebra. All these fractures appear to have been sustained during their vigorous lives and all show definite signs of healing.

One unidentified adult male exhibited a severe, but healed, fracture of the right distal femur resulting in a large callus formation in which the distal end was displaced medially to the proximal shaft (Fig. 3.14; Barbian and Sledzik 2005). The fracture was extensive enough to have required binding to heal, most likely from a medical specialist. The resulted shortening of the leg certainly caused a pronounced walking limp and the leg's rearrangement developed into secondary osteoarthritis at both the distal and proximal ends of the femur. Mobility would have been a strenuous activity. None of the females in the family exhibited any noticeable fractures, indicative of domestic daily life as opposed to agricultural fieldwork. Since none of the skeletal elements with fractures exhibited nutritional deficiencies (*i.e.*, osteoporosis) or osteomyelitis, it seems most likely that these fractures were the result of accidental trauma or occupational stress associated with farming.

Surprisingly, the Bulkeley skeletons showed no evidence of communicable diseases such as tuberculosis, which was widespread in New England during those years. However, two cases of degenerative joint disease may warrant a diagnosis other than osteoarthritis. Daniel and Joshua Bulkeley both older men, exhibited skeletal fusion indicative of diffuse idiopathic skeletal hyperostosis (DISH), which results from the ossification of the spinal

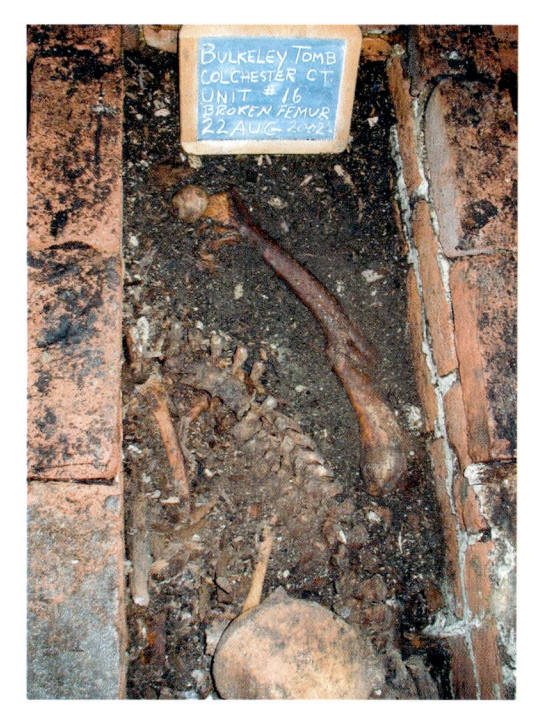

Fig. 3.14. Right femur of unidentified adult male in situ from the Bulkeley Tomb showing severe distal fracture (Photo: John J. Spaulding).

ligaments without any associated intervertebral disk disease. While the cause of DISH remains unknown, it is rarely detected before 40 years of age and is more common in males than females. In addition, one unidentified adult male exhibited fused sacrum and innominate (pelvis) bones and may be the result of ankylosing spondylitis (AS), which is a progressive, non-infectious inflammatory disorder in which the connective tissue of the spine and sacroiliac joint calcify (Bastis 2006, 40–1; Vigorita 2008, 666). Again, the nature of these pathological conditions suggests everyday traumatic injury consistent with middle or older age and a lifetime of hard physical labor (Olivieri *et al.* 2009).

While economically prosperous, Gershom and his family were undoubtedly hardy, physical laborers as demonstrated from their skeletal conditions. The bones of every male are robust, showing well-developed protuberances at points of muscle attachment with thick bone density. If anything, the family's wealth is demonstrated in exhibiting no signs of nutritional stress on their teeth (no indications of enamel hypoplasia or Harris' lines); they ate well and often.

Dental health of this time period was typically atrocious. Food preparation resulted in a high consumption of processed grains and sugars leading to elevated rates of caries and periodontal disease. Few people ever saw a dentist or even owned a toothbrush. Yet the Bulkeley family exhibited few cavities in the extant dentition observed. This could be indicative of a cary-resistant population, or more likely, that the Bulkeleys were receiving professional dental care of some sort. This may also be demonstrated in the high percentage of ante-mortem (before death) tooth lost suggesting that infected teeth may have been pulled, hence providing a lower percentage of observable caries. Professional health care can be observed in Epaphroditus Bulkeley's two dental partials and in another unidentified family member's gold fillings (Bastis 2006, 44).

The family's life actuary statistics reflect similar demographic estimates encountered in other cemetery populations from this time period (Daly 2002). The demographic breakdown from the Bulkeley Tomb shows an increased number of children and older people being buried, with fewer deaths occurring during middle age. Deciphering ages into decades of life, the highest number of deaths (9) occurred during childhood and adolescence, followed by family members dying at over 60 years of age (12). Over 68% (21 out of 31) of the individual skeletons identified are either children or seniors (Bastis 2006). And, of course, Sarah Trumbull Welles Bulkeley died in her 96th year! Of the 30 adult burials, 19 are male and 11 female (Bastis 2006).

Coffin material studies consisted of wood and hardware analyses. Lucinda McWeeney, an archaeobotantist, identified wood species from coffin lids and sideboards, concluding that the majority of the coffins were constructed from white pine (McWeeney 2005). However, most of the earliest coffins dating from 1775 to 1810 were constructed from mahogany, tulip polar, maple or cherry, all relatively expensive hardwoods. Interestingly, some of the coffins were made up of an assortment of woods. That is, the footboard, headboard and bottom/top boards of the same coffin were constructed from different species of wood. There were cut marks on some of the bottom boards suggesting that they had other uses before being assembled as coffins. In addition, eight coffins were painted red or black and another four had a shellac finish. Little symbolism should be read into the colors red and black. Rather than symbolizing death and blood, these were relatively inexpensive paints of the time period and red was often used as a varnish and not the final coating. Coffin hardware consisted of 44 metal handles and numerous nails. Ross Harper (2005) found that five of the brass coffin handles were actually from furniture pulls that were converted to carry coffins. Eight handles were hammered out of pewter (Fig. 3.15). While material culture identified from the tomb matches expectations of a relatively wealthy family being able to afford elaborate coffins for their deceased loved ones, the recycling of wooden furniture and building planks converted into coffins hardware and boards also suggests that the family were good "Yankees" in that they wasted little and reused what they had even for the housing of their dead.

Other artifacts recovered from the tomb include a brass hair comb, the soles of a pair of shoes, a cast-iron gate finial and a complete 1820s English Staffordshire saucer plate, which is the only artifact we could associate from within a specific coffin (Burial #28), while the others were found amid collapsed debris (Bellantoni and Spaulding 2002). No sign of clothing was discovered on any of the burials. Before mass production of clothing in the mid-1800s, clothes were hand-woven and even wealthy families rarely buried their dead with such expensive and needed items, choosing to pass their clothing on to heirs in the family. We assume that all the Bulkeleys in the tomb were buried in shrouds, though very few shroud pins survived.

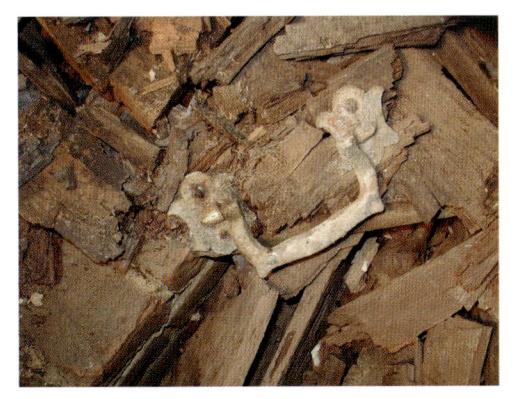

Fig. 3.15. Coffin hardware handle in situ as recovered from the Bulkeley Tomb (Photo: John J. Spaulding).

Fig. 3.16. Bulkeley descendants and friends attend reburial ceremony, 11 October 2003 (Photo: John J. Spaulding).

Fig. 3.17. Restored tomb of the Gershom Bulkeley and his Descendants, Colchester Burial Ground, Colchester, Connecticut (Photo: Brian Meyer).

As forensic and materials analyses were ongoing, the Gardner-Bulkeley Cemetery Association, Inc., who financially supported the study, approved the donation of five coffin lids recovered from the tomb to be retained by the Colchester Historical Society, Connecticut Historical Society and the Connecticut State Museum of Natural History. The Maryland Archaeological Conservation Laboratories, Inc. was contracted to conserve five of the lids, including those of Abigail Robbins Bulkeley, Peter Bulkeley, Judith Worthington Bulkeley, Anna Bulkeley Rogers and William Bulkeley.

****

With Peter Bulkeley acting as master of ceremonies, over 40 descendants attended the reburial ceremony at Colchester's Ancient Burial Ground on 11 October 2003. The remains of their ancestors disinterred for forensic analyses were reinterred into the newly renovated Gershom Bulkeley Tomb. Our team placed Bulkeley family skeletal remains in Ziegler cases, which are used to transporting human remains without a coffin/casket, positioned as close as possible to their original placements inside the tomb. The marble epitaph fragments that set off the whole project were also placed inside the crypt. As at the Pitkin Tomb, a newly engraved stone with the names of each Bulkeley family member identified was commemorated in front

3. The Tomb of Gershom Bulkeley and His Descendants

THE TOMB OF GERSHOM BULKELEY (1708-1788) AND
HIS DESCENDENTS WAS REDISCOVERED IN MAY OF 2002.
RESTORATION WAS COMPLETED IN 2003 AND THE REMAINS
OF THE BULKELEY FAMILY MEMBERS WERE THEN REINTERRED.

BULKELEYS

PETER	1712 - 1798	JOHN	1759 - 1788
ABIGAIL	1714 - 1793	WILLIAM	1761 - 1801
JOHN	1738 - 1807	ASA	1774 - 1804
JOSHUA	1741 - 1821	GEORGE	1780 - 1811
JUDITH	1742 - 1801	HARRIET	1785 - 1808
MARY	1742 - 1811	GERSHOM	1788 - 1832
LOIS	1742 - 1812	EPAPHRODITUS	1791 - 1817
DANIEL	1744 - 1810	JERUSHA	1800 - 1804
DAVID	1749 - 1812	OLIVER	1802 - 1813
RHODA	1750 - 1807	BENJAMIN	1806 - 1819
ROGER	1751 - 1819	RICHARD	1824 - 1826
	HANNAH	AGE 76	

SARAH BULKELEY WELLES	1702 - 1798
CHAUNCEY WELLES	1744 - 1810
GERSHOM TAINTOR	1765 - 1775
JOHN WORTHINGTON	1773 - 1806
SARAH BULKELEY ROGERS	1779 - 1821
ANNA ROGERS	1802 - 1805

Fig. 3.18. Engraved tombstone with names of Bulkeley ancestors identified within the Gershom Bulkeley Tomb (Photo: John J. Spaulding).

of and over the refilled stairway of the burial chamber (Fig. 3.18). For all those participating and supporting this project, our hopes are that the tomb will never be "lost" again and that "Gershom Bulkeley and his Descendants" will never be forgotten.

Chapter 4

The Tomb of His Excellency Samuel Huntington, Esq.

That done, they plac'd the carase in the tomb,
To dust and dull oblivion now resign'd,
Then turn'd the chariot tow'rd the House of the Night,
Which soon flew off, and left no trace behind.

Philip Freneau, *The House of the Night*

The funeral had all the pomp and circumstance one would expect for a Governor of the State of Connecticut, signer of the *Declaration of Independence,* contributor to the United States Constitution and Bill of Rights, past President of the Continental Congress, and revered (though forgotten) Founding Father. His Excellency, Samuel Huntington, Esquire, died on 5 January 1796 at the age of 64 and was being laid to rest 3 days later beside his beloved wife Martha, in the tomb he had built to contain his family's mortal remains in the Norwichtown Burying Ground (Fig. 4.1). The funeral procession, led by muffled drums of the Twentieth State Regiment beating a steady, slow cadence, four military companies marching with rifles reversed, over 200 military officers, noted politicians and clergy from various denominations, was most impressive and solemn (Gerlach 1976, 105). Nonetheless, certain matters did go awry.

Undertakers, in preparing the body, failed to place a sword beside Samuel as he lay in his hexagonal coffin, which was appropriate for a State Governor at that time. They rationalized their error by asserting that since Huntington always wore a "borrow'd" sword and was a man of peace, the omission was appropriate. Adding to the matter, the military guard was not permitted to fire armaments. There was to be no 21-gun salute at the grave site for fear that the new Governor's wife, who was with child, would be startled. The colonel in charge was, to say the least, not pleased, nor were the soldiers when they were not offered any liquor, as was custom, to ward off the wintry cold during the lengthy funeral process. And, when finally passing Samuel's coffin through the narrow opening of the tomb, the pallbearers mistakenly brought the coffin in head first instead of feet first. Once inside the compact crypt and the mistake realized, Samuel's box had to be spun 180° so his head was oriented toward the entranceway, requiring a bit of jostling within the restricted tomb to place him appropriately upon the upper, left side shelf (Bushnell 1796). Not necessarily the best executed send-off, but by the end of the day, Samuel was finally laid to rest on the stone shelf across from his much-loved wife Martha.

The brick and stone masonry tomb Samuel had constructed into the south facing aspect of a small hill in the burying ground immediately behind his house on East Town Street, Norwich, Connecticut was relatively undersized compared to the Pitkin and Bulkeley burial chambers, which were built to house the remains of their rapidly growing number of descendants. The Huntington marriage was childless. However, when Hannah, Samuel's brother Joseph's wife, died in 1771, Samuel and Martha adopted and raised their niece and nephew, 6-year-old Samuel (his namesake) and 2-year-old Frances, as part of their household. Within a year of these adoptions, the couple would also take in 11-year old Mason Fitch Cogswell, the motherless child of the Rev. James Cogswell, who succeeded Martha's father, Ebenezer Devotion as pastor at Scotland, and suddenly the Huntington household grew to three children (Waugh 1968, 20). Hence, the tomb was built with the sense that only five burials, at most, would be required.

Fig. 4.1. His Excellency, Samuel Huntington, Esq. (Credit: National Portrait Gallery, Smithsonian Institution).

The Huntington Tomb is a classic "mound" tomb with a subterranean chamber formed by a single-arch brick vault (Fig. 4.2). A buttress, made of rough stone masonry, wraps around the brickwork to form an inverted letter "U" supporting the arch. The entranceway has a small granite stairway that descends to a door, which was filled over with dirt and bricks at the center of the front wall once the tomb was closed. A granite lintel sits horizontally over the door and the bottom step into the tomb rests above the earthen floor of the vault. Two white marble plaques were placed in the center of the front wall (Fig. 4.3). The upper contains the main inscriptions; the lower states "Signer of the Declaration of Independence" and may have been added later.

Inside the tomb, floor-to-ceiling height is 7 ft (2.13 m) and the interior measures a mere 7 ft (2.13 m) wide and 11 ft (3.35 m) in length to the back north wall. All inner surfaces are washed with a white-colored lime and sand stucco. There are

Fig. 4.2. The Tomb of Samuel and Martha Huntington, Norwichtown Cemetery, Norwich, CT, prior to restoration in 2003 (Photo: John J. Spaulding).

Fig. 4.3. Marble epitaph, exterior south wall of the Huntington Tomb (Photo: Brian Meyer).

4. The Tomb of His Excellency Samuel Huntington, Esq.

Fig. 4.4. The interior of the Huntington Tomb showing two horizontal rows of stone slabs used to support coffins (Photo: John J. Spaulding).

Fig. 4.5. Lateral View of the Huntington Tomb (facing east) showing the front façade collapsing from the body of the tomb (Photo: John J. Spaulding).

two horizontal rows of projecting flat fieldstones that are cantilevered out of three interior walls toward the center of the tomb. These stone slabs supported wooden coffins keeping them from lying on the damp earthen floor and are unique from the usual brick partitions seen in most New England tombs, such as in the Pitkin and Bulkeley crypts (Fig. 4.4).

These architectural elements were part of the original construction in the 1790s. However, additional bricks other than those from the colonial era suggest that a later restoration was attempted in the late 19th century. A major concern, even then, was the outward movement of the front, bricked south façade pulling away from the main body of the tomb, which eventually opened an 8 in (20 cm) gap (Fig. 4.5). This was probably caused by the pressure of the soil from behind the wall and seems to have been a chronic weak point in the structure since its original construction. The tomb was seriously in need of another restoration by the beginning of the 21st century (Myjer 2003).

As part of the rebuilding process, the Office of State Archaeology was contacted by the project's renovation consultants and the Norwich Historical Society in June, 2003, for technical assistance when initial inspection by the contractors peering through the crevice breach noted wooden fragments of the original coffins and several scattered human skeletal remains that would need to be cleared prior to the tomb's restoration.

Our involvement as State Archaeologist was three-fold: To recover the physical remains of Samuel and Martha Huntington and any associated funerary objects which would be temporarily transferred to a local funeral director while construction activities were underway, and, once completed, assist with their return to the restored tomb for reburial; to conduct forensic analyses on the remains and identify artifacts housed within the tomb; and, finally, to assess any vandalism that may have occurred in the past and affirm or refute rumors that the tomb had been broken into during the early 20th century.

****

Perhaps the best epitaph for Samuel Huntington is "The Forgotten Founding Father." He was not the General of the Armies as was George Washington; he did not have the flamboyant personality of Benjamin Franklin; he was not a prolific writer like John Adams; and he would never be considered the Renaissance man that was Thomas Jefferson. Compared to these political and intellectual giants, Samuel Huntington is the least remembered, yet he worked closely with all of them and, more importantly, he held their utmost respect and confidence. Unlike John and Abigail Adams, who wrote down every blessed thought and opinion they ever entertained, we only have six extant personal letters from Samuel Huntington and those consist mostly of business and political dealings. Hence, we know little about his personal thinking, though his attitudes and fingerprints and signatures are inscribed all over the most important documents of the nascent United States of America.

And, of course, Samuel had humble origins. The first Puritan immigrant of the family was Simon Huntington, who set sail from Yarmouth, England onboard the *Elizabeth Bonaventure* in 1633 with his wife, Margaret, and their children. Unfortunately, Simon died of smallpox during the voyage to America and was buried at sea. His widow and four surviving offspring arrived in Boston and made residence in Roxbury, Massachusetts, where they sought fellowship in the Church of Christ. Within a couple of years, Margaret remarried to Thomas Stoughton, who moved his new family to Windsor, Connecticut (Huntington Family Association 1915, 11).

Simon, Jr, who was the eldest child and only 4 years old when the family came to New England, married Sarah Clarke in 1653 and together they were one of the earliest settlers of Norwich, Connecticut (Huntington Family Association 1915, 419), where Simon became a large landholder. Simon and Sarah would have ten children, the fourth born was Joseph Huntington, Samuel's paternal grandfather. Joseph Huntington was the first of his family born in Norwich in September 1661. He married Rebecca Adgate in 1687 and moved to Windham, Connecticut, where he was chosen deacon of the First Church in 1729. Joseph and Rebecca's second child, Nathaniel was born on 1 September 1691 and he would marry Mehetable Thurston of Bristol, Rhode Island on 28 February 1723 (Huntington Family Association 1915, 543). They would remain together for 45 years.

Samuel Huntingon's Puritan parents, Nathaniel and Mehetable, were not poor by any means, but neither were they affluent. They were common farmers, though they had ten extraordinarily uncommon children, with Samuel, their fourth child, the most so. Samuel was born on 5 July 1731 in the Scotland section of Windham, Connecticut, or so we think. The uncertainty results from an inkblot that obscures his birth entry in the Windham Vital Records. The date of Samuel's birth is shown as "July 731", with the blot obscuring the middle part of the date rendering it illegible (Waugh 1968, 7). The 3rd or the 5th of July 1731 have both been accepted dates by historians. Whichever one recognized, it is thought provoking to note that Huntington might have missed by one day (either way) having been born on the 4th of July!

Nathaniel wanted him to become a farmer like himself and apprenticed him out to a cooper to learn the trade of making barrel hoops and staves, but the teenaged Samuel found the cooperage life unsatisfying and sought another career path. When the family minister, Rev. Ebenezer Devotion, offered young Samuel the unrestricted use of his personal library, the teenager taught himself Latin and, when taking an interest in law, educated himself in jurisprudence (Waugh 1968, 12). Two local Windham lawyers recognized the budding talent of young Huntington and further offered their counseling and law books for him to study. These mentors and his self-training regime culminated in Samuel being admitted to the bar by 1754 soon opening his own law practice in Norwich where he lived for the rest of his life.

Samuel was not only paying attention to his budding career in jurisprudence, but he was also paying a great deal of attention to Rev. Devotion's eldest daughter, Martha. It is likely that they had some form of "agreement" prior before his leaving for Norwich to immerse himself in his law practice. Samuel and Martha married on 17 April 1761, in a ceremony performed by her father. They remained "uncommonly happy" for the rest of their lives (Strong 1796, 16; Waugh 1968, 16).

Before long Huntington established himself as a favored local lawyer serving as the Norwich town attorney, tax collector, and Justice of the Peace, offices that eventually accelerated him to the colonial government in Hartford. By 1764, he was appointed to represent Norwich in the Connecticut Colony General Assembly, where he made his dissenting opinions clear when Britain evoked the Stamp Act in 1765, endangering the rights of his fellow colonists. Huntington considered himself loyal to the King, but as tensions grew he fell more in political alignment with the "Sons of Liberty," eventually becoming a leading voice in Connecticut's response to the Revolution (Huntington Family Association, 1915, 546; Waugh 1968, 19).

As the colonies grew closer to rebellion, Huntington's career began to steamroll. In 1773, Samuel was appointed King's Attorney for the Connecticut Court, but resigned the succeeding year when relationships with Great Britain continued to deteriorate and, in good conscience, felt he could no longer effectively represent the King in the Crown's Court. By 1775, at the age of 43 years, he was chosen to stand for Connecticut at the Second Continental Congress being formed in Philadelphia, serving there when the "Shot Heard Round the World" was fired at the Battle of Concord, Massachusetts. Samuel was appointed to the Council of Safety, also known as the Committee of War (Chorlton 2011, 206–206), to assist Connecticut Governor Trumbull on colonial affairs associated with the coming conflict. Though still hoping for peace, Huntington and fellow members of the Continental Congress recognized that the colonies could no longer owe allegiance to the King, especially after George III proclaimed them to be in revolt against his monarchy. Huntington would vote "Aye" to formally approve the

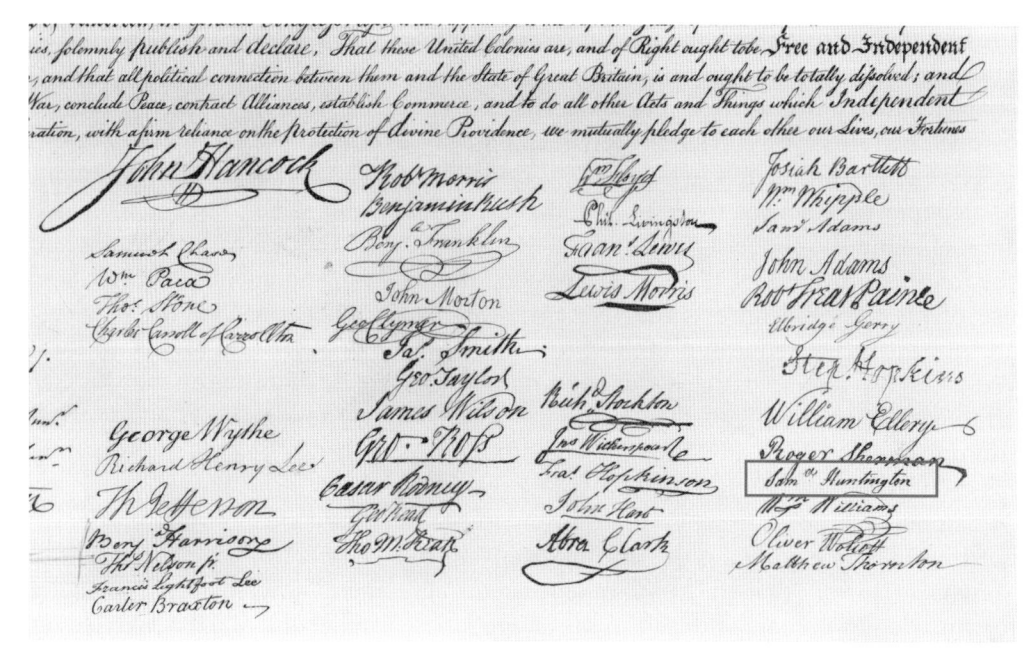

Fig. 4.6. Declaration of Independence with Samuel Huntington's signature highlighted (Credit: National Archives with thanks to James Hall).

Declaration of Independence, which he signed in the lower right side of the document knowing full well the penalties of open rebellion to the King (Fig. 4.6).

Three years later, when John Jay resigned as President of the Continental Congress to become Minister to Spain, Samuel Huntington was unanimously voted to fill the vacancy (Cholton 2011, 211). Unanimously!! How was this self-effacing Connecticut Yankee acceptable to *all* representatives of Congress, North and South, to such an important position at a time of crisis? And do not for a moment think that there was not already regional strife among the colonies at that formative time. Yet all representatives were confident that this self-taught lawyer from rural Connecticut could provide the leadership Congress demanded in the advancing political and military struggle. What did they, to a man, see in Huntington that made his election undisputed?

Adjectives written at the time to describe Samuel include words like stable, dignified, diplomatic, methodical, steady, fearless, energetic, intelligent, fair, logical, calm, honorable, integrity, and a man of few words (Strong 1796; Waugh 1968; Gerlach 1976). Somehow he found a way to keep his eye on the ball and not allow regional factionalism or heated argument to cloud his decision-making. He was a diplomat's diplomat; the right man, in the right place, for the right job and he would hold the presidency of the Continental Congress and the Confederation Congress longer (1 year, 285 days) than any other individual in their 14-year histories.

4. The Tomb of His Excellency Samuel Huntington, Esq.

Long enough to be President when the Articles of Confederation were ratified on 1 March 1781, at the very birth of the United States of America. Hence, some historians (McCabe 2004, 1) and family descendants would argue that Samuel Huntington was, in fact, the first President of the United States, not George Washington, 8 years later! Of course, Huntington was the first *Congressional* President of the United States (there would be nine others to follow), while Washington was the first Constitutional *Executive* President. No matter these distinctions, there is no denying that Samuel Huntington was an absolutely essential public figure in the founding of the country. One speculates, as fragile as the developing nation was at that time, how things might have turned out differently had it not been for Huntington's tactful leadership.

With his health declining due to smallpox infection, Samuel reluctantly resigned as President of Congress in July 1781 (Chorlton 2011, 217–18). His fellow representatives delayed the vote for a successor for 2 months hoping that Huntington's health would improve and he could resume his responsibilities as chief executive. But his lack of strength required that Congress accept his resignation, which they reluctantly did (Huntington Family Association 1915, 548). Though Huntington was re-elected the following year by the people of Connecticut to once again represent them in Congress, he could not travel and did not attend sessions. Nonetheless, regaining his health and being called on to serve yet again in 1783, Samuel journeyed to Princeton, where Congress was then meeting, and gave it one last try. He would refuse re-election in 1774, returning home to Norwich to enjoy retirement.

Well, not exactly retirement. He was held in such high esteem among the citizens of state that he was overwhelmingly elected Connecticut Governor in 1786 and, then, re-elected an amazing ten times (governors served 1-year terms back then), functioning as the first Governor of the State under the new Federal Constitution. Connecticut became the 5th State to ratify the charter, whose endorsement Huntington strongly supported. By his death in 1796, there would be a number of "firsts" in Samuel Huntington's résumé in the midst of the growing nation.

Like William Pitkin III before him, Samuel would lose his wife while serving as governor, and like Pitkin, he, too, would expire while still in office. After 33 years of marriage, Martha Huntington died on 3 June 1794, following a short, though "distressing" illness at the age of 55. She had been by Samuel's side the whole time, maintaining an organized household, hosting parties and dinners for some of the great men of the era and raising three adopted children. Martha was venerated by the people of Connecticut in her own right; often the subject of rousing cheers when she entered a public space. His adopted niece, Fanny, would take over the household responsibilities for the aging Samuel, but his health – an issue for the last 20 years of his life – began to deteriorate further after Martha died (Waugh 1968, 39). Samuel Huntington followed his wife to the grave 2 years later, on 5 January 1796, at the age of 64 from "dropsy of the chest" (Huntington Family Association 1915, 550) and "without any painful struggles" (Gerlach 1976, 105). He would be interred into the small family tomb across the center aisle from her. Together, they would remain the only mortal remains residing within.

****

The Huntington Tomb is located in the "new" section of the Old Burying Ground in Norwichtown, Connecticut. From the main entrance, travel the dirt road passing a monument on your left dedicated to 20 French Soldiers who served under General Lafayette during the War for Independence and who had died of smallpox while touring through the town. The oldest section (18th century) of the burying ground lies ahead where you will find the tombstone of Benedict Arnold's mother, Hannah. The dirt road will extend to the north on your left and across a bridge spanning a small brook to the "new" section (19th century). To your immediate left as you cross the bridge will stand the largest monument in the graveyard, the brick and stone Tomb of Samuel and Martha Huntington.

When the bricks and packed soil sealing the diminutive front entrance were removed, I was the first person to re-enter the Huntington Tomb on Monday, 20 October 2003, as part of the initial stage of the $31,000 restoration project. It was a sunny, crisp New England autumn morning. The enveloping hardwood trees were reaching their colorful seasonal peaks and with street traffic and neighboring houses at a distance, the tomb was bathed by a tranquil and picturesque backdrop. While we took the time to notice the serene ambience, we were anxious to begin our work. Descending four stone steps and crouching through the small opening in the brick facade, I wondered to myself how they were able to get the coffins and pallbearers through such a tight doorway. There was little room to maneuver even my slight body through the entrance.

Employing heavy battery-powered lights to see through the tomb's dimness, we readily observed that the interior contained deteriorating wooden coffins of only two individuals and that organic preservation of their skeletal remains was exceedingly poor. The pulling away of the southern wall from the tomb's main body resulted in a crevice that exposed the interior to animals and weathering factors. Bottom coffin boards had maintained their original placement balancing on stone slabs, but as the wooden coffins desiccated and broke apart, wood and skeletal elements occupying the gaps between the fieldstones, tumbled to the floor. Hence, we found disarticulated skeletons with some bones still balancing on the stone slabs and others collapsed to the dirt floor underneath. Fortunately, since Samuel and Martha were laid to rest on the top of two separate rows of stone slabs on each side of the tomb, their remains were not commingled on the floor, but rested separately below their respective placements.

The hexagonal, cherry wood coffin of Martha Huntington was laid across three flat fieldstones on the eastern (right) wall of the tomb and positioned in a north–south orientation, head to the south. Overall organic preservation was meager and not all skeletal elements were represented since those with lesser bone density like ribs and the scapula had decomposed. We began by recording and mapping Martha's remains from the foot of the coffin and proceeded systematically towards the head region. Her right tibia (shinbone) was extremely decomposed, as was surprisingly the right proximal femur, since these two elements have excellent bone density, yet they were disintegrating badly. Signs of extension arthritis were exhibited in the right knee joint, including the patella (knee bone). Surviving phalanges (fingers) of the hands were laid out over the pelvic area, though not crossed. The pelvis, however, had collapsed between the slabs and lay on the floor beneath. Cranial vault elements were recovered but were porous and fragile with none of the thin bones of the craniofacial area preserved (Bellantoni 2003).

Martha Huntington's bones exhibited a high degree of adipocere staining, which is often referred to as grave, or corpse, wax. It appears as a milky, soapy texture formed on the bones due to a process called saponification, developing when body fat is exposed to anaerobic bacteria in a damp environment. Adipocere can actually help preserve the bone and may have been a factor of the moisture content in the tomb, the sealed coffin and the funeral clothing she wore on her upper body (Pfeiffer *et al.* 1998). This same chemical breakdown was also observed, though to a lesser degree, on Samuel's skeletal remains.

A shroud pin was recovered from the area of the greater trochanter of the right femur. Two coffin hinges were also found, as well as fragments of a two-piece coffin lid. The split lid and hinges allowed for the head portion of the coffin to be lifted to view the face during the funeral without having to hoist the entire top board. A delicate thread of ribbon was tied with a bow and recorded in the neck region, an ornament that would have been visible with the upper lid open during the funeral (Fig. 4.7). A material that appeared to be wood shavings was recovered from under her cranium and included some textile fragments, all of which may have been part of a pillow for Martha to rest her head upon (Bellantoni 2003).

The remains of Samuel Huntington were located on the west side of the tomb also lying in a north–south direction, head towards the south doorway. The overall length of the crumbling cherry wood coffin was measured at 73 in (1.85 m). Samuel was laid out over three fieldstones with the end slab supporting the foot of the coffin, the middle slab supporting the femurs/pelvis and the upper chest area on the head slab. Similar to Martha, the hands were in the pelvic region, but not crossed. His overall organic preservation was only slightly better than that of Martha.

Fig. 4.7. The ribbon tied in a bow on the remains of Martha Huntington (Photo: John J. Spaulding).

Foot bones and the patella had collapsed between the spaces of the slabs and were recovered resting on the stones of the lower row having been arrested there before hitting the ground. The left arm (humerus and radius), dentition and rib fragments were also recorded upon the head and middle slabs. The radial tuberosity was extremely robust, suggesting an individual with relatively muscular forearms. The posterior distal portion of the femur exhibited "coffin wear" erosion of the cortical surface due to abrasion from lying on the bottom board, as did his right calcaneus (heel bone) (Pokines and Baker 2013, 90–1). The cranial vault, minus facial elements, was recovered in one piece, collapsing from slabs above. Endo-cranial sutures were completely obliterated suggesting older age. Extensive mouse nesting was apparent in the vacant cranial vault (Bellantoni 2003).

At the foot of the coffin, we found an iron handle with hardware nails still protruding from apertures that would have been secured into the end of the hardwood coffin for pallbearers to grasp. Another metal coffin handle was recovered from an undetermined sideboard. A portion of the headboard, with the joint and portion of the left sideboard together were also retrieved but did not possess a metal handle. The coffin lid was in two parts with hinges similar to that identified on Martha's coffin lid. Several shroud pins were also recovered, suggesting that Samuel was buried naked with a sheet covering his body. We found no traces of boots, buckles or buttons. Both coffins appear to have similarities in their hexagonal design and two-piece lids. The lone exception was that Samuel's coffin had metal handles, where Martha's exhibited no evidence of any hardware other than nails and hinges and that Martha was dressed from the waist up and Samuel appears to have only had a shroud adorning his body.

While the funerary objects recovered spoke to the style of coffins, which were state-of-the-art funeral furniture in the late 18th century, the most interesting artifacts located in the tomb were two brass medallions that had been originally attached to the lids of each coffin. Residing on one of the slabs aligned to Samuel's lower chest/abdomen, we located a corroded, but legible, oval silver-plated nameplate with four puncture holes (Fig. 4.8). The medallion read:

> *His Excellency*
> *Samuel Huntington, Esq.*
> *Governor of the State of Connecticut*
> *was born July 16th AD 1731*
> *and died January 5th AD 1796*
> *aged 64 years.*

Note the date of birth. Remember our confusion due to the inkblot stains of the archived public records? Now, we seemed to have evidence that Samuel died on 16 July, instead of the fifth as historians suspected. So, at first we thought we had some hard data to clear up the birthday mystery, but not so. Both dates actually refer to the same day! In 1752, the British adopted the Gregorian calendar to synchronize their former Julian calendar with that of Catholic Europe. So, to catch up, they skipped 11

4. The Tomb of His Excellency Samuel Huntington, Esq.

Fig. 4.8. The brass nameplate of His Excellency Governor Samuel Huntington (Photo: John J. Spaulding).

days forward, similar to our hourly changes to Daylight Savings Time. As a result, many people adjusted their birthdate 11 days ahead to conform to the new calendar and be able to celebrate their next birthday 365 days later. George Washington is probably the most prominent example of changing their birth date to conform to the Gregorian calendar. We can assume that Samuel Huntington may have done the same thing, adjusting his birthday from 5 July to 16 July. At least now we can be relatively certain that the original Windham archive refers to 5 July and not the third of the month.

Martha Huntington's nameplate had collapsed to the dirt floor (Fig. 4.9) and was recovered underneath the slabs and amongst her scattered skeletal remains. When cleaned, it read:

> *Martha Huntington*
> *Consort of Samuel Huntington,*
> *Governor of this State. Dyed*
> *June 3rd 1794. Aged 55*
> *(Noting that "Consort" was the equivalent of "wife" in the 18th century)*

While negative evidence is unacceptable in archaeology, we found no indication inside the tomb that vandalism had occurred. The array of skeletal remains and coffin

Fig. 4.9. The brass nameplate of Martha Huntington (Photo: John J. Spaulding).

wood and hardware on the stone slabs and the dirt floor beneath were from natural decomposition and collapse. Understanding that State Governors in that time period were buried with swords, the historical account of its omission was also important in our interpretation. There simply were no signs of plunder.

Forensically, there was not a lot to go by, but probably the most surprising thing about Samuel Huntington was the degree of robusticity exhibited in his skeletal remains, suggesting a degree of muscular strength not usually associated with the lifestyle of a lawyer and diplomat, but rather of a blacksmith or farmer. Perhaps his early training in the agrarian life that his father had wished him to take up as a career may have resulted in the muscularity observed. He did not show signs of extensive arthritis as Martha did. He did, however, demonstrate stress from a possible dislocation of his left shoulder. He stood an estimated 5 ft 8 in (1.72 m) based on tibia length formulae. Only three teeth survived (mandibular molars) and show moderate-to-extensive wear on the occlusal surfaces with no caries present. Since smallpox leaves limited visible signatures on the skeleton we did not observe signs of osteomyelitis variolosa on any of the long bones so could not confirm or deny his chronic condition to the disease (Jackes 1982).

Martha Huntington exhibited severe secondary osteoarthritic condition in her right knee, as well as a bone spur on the right medial malleolus (foot bone), which could have developed due to trauma. Had she been alive today, Martha would have been an excellent candidate for knee replacement surgery. In the 1790s, she could only "grin and bear" the pain of her daily attempts at walking. Her height is estimated as

5 ft 7 in (1.70 m) based on tibia length. Overall, we come to appreciate the difficulties of everyday life at that time even among the most prominent people.

Assisted by University of Connecticut graduate students Mark Macauda and Cara Roure, along with volunteers from the Friends of the Office of State Archaeology, Inc. (FOSA) including Dave Cooke and John Spaulding, each of the skeletal elements, coffin materials and soil samples was carefully bagged, labeled, and laid gently into a galvanized Ziegler transfer case. The remains were transported by Church & Allen Funeral Services of Norwich, where they awaited the tomb restoration and assembly into new coffins for reburial. The case was draped with the American flag and conveyed in a black hearse from the burying ground to the funeral home.

Once all human remains and material culture were removed from the tomb's interior, the structural restoration work began. The essential step in reconditioning the Huntington Tomb involved the dismantling and rebuilding of the front wall that had pulled away from the rest of the tomb in order to correct the inherent mechanical problems of the original design. The interior of the tomb remained the same, though brackets allowing for some additional mechanical support and the filling of small cracks and fissures in the stucco masonry were applied (Fig. 4.10).

Fig. 4.10. Huntington Tomb restoration process, front wall removed (Photo: John J. Spaulding).

Using only hand tools, the front wall was taken apart brick-by-brick, separating the original colonial pieces from ones that were replaced during the late 19th-century renovations, with the former incorporated into the new façade where appropriate. The front wall was rebuilt using a soft lime mortar (Myjer 2003).

****

Silence overcoming the more than 300 people attending the re-interment ceremony for Samuel and Martha Huntington contrasted with the loud cracking of rifles booming a 21-gun salute from the First Company, Governor's Foot Guard throughout the Old Burying Ground (Fig. 4.11). William Stanley, president of the Norwich Historical Society and leader of the restoration effort, wanted to ensure that Samuel Huntington and his wife, Martha, were being returned to their restored tomb with full military honors and a ceremony befitting the "first President of the United States" (Foster 2003).

Along with the Governor's Foot Guard, members of the Samuel Huntington Chapter of the Sons of the American Revolution, U.S. Naval personnel, state and local police,

Fig. 4.11. The Governor's First Foot Guard carrying the period coffin of Samuel Huntington during reburial in the Huntington Tomb (Photo: John J. Spaulding).

delegates from the Governor's office, U.S. Representative Rob Simmons, U.S. Senator Christopher Dodd's wife Jackie, as well as Mohegan Nation tribal ambassadors, historians and members of the Huntington family spoke and led a procession following the contemporary flag-draped caskets of Samuel and Martha Huntington, ascending the hill to the newly restored tomb. Revolutionary War re-enactors and the public lined the procession route. Gov. John G. Rowland declared the date, 24 November 2003, "Samuel Huntington Day" throughout Connecticut.

Church & Allen Funeral Services gratuitously donated two colonial period hexagonal wooden coffins for the remains of Samuel and Martha to be reburied in. Secured to the top coffin boards, in what would have been their original placements, were the two original silver nameplates we recovered and conserved from the tomb excavation. The caskets were draped with American flags and driven to the cemetery in two separate black hearses.

While I was able to glimpse a portion of the opening ceremonies and listen to some of the remarks, I missed the procession since I was required inside the tomb, positioned to receive both coffins and return them in their original locations on the upper stone slabs. The Governor's Foot Guard, adorned with tall fur hats, served as pallbearers. Approaching the tomb, they aligned the sides of each coffin removing and folding the respective American flags with appropriate care and ceremony. The flags were presented to Channing M. Huntington II, a family descendant.

The Foot Guard pallbearers then approached the tomb's narrow steps leading down to the crypt's close-fitting entrance where Dave Cooke and I stood poised inside to receive the coffins. And this time we made sure that both coffins came in feet first, so we would not have to rotate them inside the tomb as they did during Samuel's 1796 burial. As expected, the coffins were barely able to pass through the narrow opening and there was a bit of difficulty transferring them from the Foot Guard to the two of us. Nonetheless, together Dave and I were able to support the weight and place them onto their appropriate shelves in the orientations as we discovered them (Fig. 4.12).

The re-interment ceremony had much of the pomp and circumstance that Samuel's original burial had in 1796, though without events going awry. Still, I do not remember the Foot Guard receiving their quantity of rum! And this time, once the Huntingtons were secured in the tomb, the Governor sanctioned a 21-gun salute ending with the solemn call of "Taps" resonating throughout the burying ground.

Fig. 4.12. The new period coffin of Samuel Huntington returned to the stone shelf, interior, Huntington Tomb (Photo: John J. Spaulding).

Fig. 4.13. Samuel Huntington Tomb restoration (Photo: Brian Meyer).

The tomb restoration, supported by a grant from the R.S. Gernon Trust of Fleet Bank, was a major success. The burial monument kept its original 18th-century style and appearance, though with improved structural support (Fig. 4.13). Newly placed stone steps now lead to the tomb entrance where once it was simply an eroded grassy incline. Everyone seemed pleased as we hoped were Samuel and Martha, once more returned to their ultimate resting place and for at least a few moments given the tribute and honor deserving of a Founding Father, even if a forgotten one.

One final story: The organizers of the reburial ceremony felt that once the observances were finished and Samuel and Martha were placed back into their private tomb, it would be a fitting token for Congressional and Senate delegates as well as donors of the restoration project to be given an opportunity to lay individual bricks sealing up the entranceway for, hopefully, the final time. And a nice gesture it was. However, while Dave and I were putting things in final order inside the tomb, we heard chinking sounds radiating from the doorway. As I turned to inspect the noise, I realized that the masons and dignitaries had already begun the double-backed bricking of the entry while we were still inside! I assume they recognized my shout and were not startled thinking that it emanated from Samuel or Martha!

****

Samuel Huntington's tomb was not the first presidential burial chamber to require restoration. Though buried almost 100 years after Samuel, President Ulysses S. Grant's immense tomb in New York City underwent restoration less than 50 years after his burial in 1885. Grant's Tomb endured a second rehabilitation in the 1990s after his descendants threatened to move his remains for lack of the tomb's upkeep. And, as recently as 2019, a third restoration was in needed to further repairs due to continual vandalism and structural rotting. Homeless people often use the tomb as a refuge in Riverside Park. Though once the biggest tourist attraction in New York City, Grant's Tomb has again been left to deteriorate due to lack of funding (Scaturro 2017; McShane 2019). Other United State Presidents that have required restoration projects to preserve their final resting places include George Washington, James Monroe, Andrew Jackson, Abraham Lincoln, James Garfield and Warren Harding.

George Washington

All arguments aside as to the first President of the United States, George Washington and his much-loved wife, (another) Martha, reside in the "New" Tomb at Mount Vernon where they are highly visited and revered by the public. Four days after his death on 14 December 1799, Washington was placed in the "Old" family brick tomb on his plantation, which was similar in general appearance to the Huntington Tomb. Acknowledging the tomb's disrepair, George left funds and specifications in his will to build a "New" crypt nearby as a final resting place for him, Martha and other family members who "may chuse (*sic*) to be entombed." (Will of George Washington 1799). The new vault, having a similar look as the old vault, was finished in 1831, when George and Martha Washington's remains were transferred there. Mount Vernon was one of the earliest historical preservation efforts in the country, and, fortunately, has led to the continual maintenance of the "New" and "Old" Tombs (www.mountvernon.org).

Abraham Lincoln

Within 30 years of his assassination, the towering tomb of Abraham Lincoln at Oak Ridge Cemetery in Springfield, Illinois, was already badly in need of repair, which persuaded the State to acquire the monument and commence restoration (Hill 2006; Lester 2015). Unlike the 1790s brick tombs of Huntington and Washington, Lincoln's colossal mausoleum had been built of sturdy stone – granite on the exterior and marble on the interior, yet it, too, was structurally failing (Challos 1997). The tomb was also the scene of an attempted grave robbing in 1876 (Roberson 1982). Besides Abraham, the tomb houses the remains of Mary Todd Lincoln, and three of Lincoln's four sons. The lone exception of the immediate family is Robert Todd Lincoln, who is buried with his wife and son at Arlington National Cemetery in Virginia.

James Monroe

For over 150 years, "patches, fillers and paint" were used to stabilize the "Birdcage" tomb of another Founding Father, President James Monroe, until 2015 when the State of Virginia announced a major restoration ahead of the bicentennial of Monroe's election as the nation's fifth president. Twenty-seven years after his death in 1831, James Monroe's remains were disinterred from Marble Cemetery, in New York City where he died, to be reinterred at Hollywood Cemetery in Richmond, Virginia, near his Belle Grove, Virginia birthplace. James Monroe's "new" granite mausoleum was erected in 1859 and protected by a cast-iron canopy (hence, the nickname, "Birdcage"). By 2015 it was corroding and necessitated dismantling, while its granite color had been darkened due to the effects of acid rain. Each piece of metal was assessed and recast or stabilized as determined and reused when possible. The granite was cleaned to bring back the original natural coloration. The $900,000 project was completed the year after it began in time for the bicentennial of his inauguration (Moomaw 2015). (Note: If you are visiting the grave of James Monroe, President John Tyler's tomb is located a few yards away.)

Andrew Jackson

President Andrew Jackson's tomb at his home, The Heritage, received extensive renovations in 1977, but also, underwent a clean up after vandals painted the word "Killer" and related profanities on the domed structure. The controversial Jackson had ordered the removal of the Cherokee Nation from the American Southeast to Indian Territory in Oklahoma resulting in the horrific Trail of Tears (Allison 2018). His remains are buried there with his wife, Rachel.

Warren Harding

Even 20th-century presidential tombs have been endangered by rapid deterioration. The tomb of Warren Harding in Marion, Ohio, was constructed in 1926, yet by the 1980s, the Ohio Historical Society had to begin a major restoration to save the structure. Harding's Tomb was built to resemble a Greek temple with an open crown and represents the last of the grandiose presidential memorials (www.hardinghome.org). Since Calvin Coolidge, most succeeding Chief Executives of the United States have chosen to be buried in much simpler plots, usually located on the grounds of their presidential libraries. John F. Kennedy is buried at Arlington National Cemetery with an eternal flame.

PART II

Tomb Vandalisms

Chapter 5

Henry Chauncey Tomb

The grave is now my home
But soon I hope to rise
Mortals behold my tomb
Keep Death before your eyes.

Epitaph of Samuel Plum, d. 1794, Miner Cemetery, Middletown, CT

The witness was wholly unreliable, having previously been arrested on drug and burglary charges. The detectives recognized that his testimony against a fellow conspirator wanted for stealing firearms from a local gun store would never hold up in a court of law alongside the cross-examination of a skilled defense lawyer. Nonetheless, during police interrogation the untrustworthy witness divulged the story of a human skull having been disposed of in a wooded area behind a car wash in Cromwell, Connecticut. His detail of the event encouraged Sgt Relford "Mitch" Ward of the Middletown Police Department to follow up with a thorough search where, in fact, a human skull was discovered in the exact location the witness described. Sergeant Ward suspected homicide and was advised to contact the State Archaeologist for technical assistance in identifying the specimen.

Upon arrival at the Middletown Police Station on 21 August 1991, the human skull was presented to me for examination in a brown paper evidence bag, labeled *Case No. 91-17738*. The specimen consisted of the cranium with no mandible present. It was readily apparent that the skull should be considered "historical" and not modern since it exhibited decomposed organic matter and breakdown of the cortical/periosteal surface. Our initial estimate was that the individual had been dead for at least 50 or more years.

Although the skull was found lying on the surface of the ground, there appeared no indication of outdoor exposure for long periods of time in an open woodland environment. Subjected to the elements, bone will dry, crack and become chalky within 2–5 years depending on local environmental conditions. In addition, there were no signs of rodent gnawing, bleaching from the sun, coloration of surrounding materials including soil and decomposing tissue, or cover by leaf litter or loose compost, all indicative of being exposed outdoors for an extended period. Most interestingly, inspection of cranial foramina (small nerve holes) and auditory canals produced no evidence of soil adherence, which we would have expected if the individual had been previously buried in the ground. As a result, we concluded that while the specimen represented an individual that had been dead for a long period of time, the skull had been maintained in an environment sealed off from contact with Connecticut's normally acidic soils, the sun and carnivore/rodent activity; and had only recently had been introduced to the unprotected environment from where it had lain (Bellantoni 1991a).

Our assessment of the specimen included estimates of sex, age, race, trauma and dental health. Biological sex determination was based on a number of diagnostic skeletal elements for sexual variation in our species. The general mass of the cranium was undersized and overall architecture was smooth; the mastoid process at the base of the skull was diminutive; the supraorbital ridge was small-to-medium; while the eye orbits were rounded, high, relatively large and with sharp superior margins. The occipital area showed no marked muscle lines or protuberances. The occipital condyle was petite, the forehead rounded in profile and the palate small and parabolic. All of these characteristics strongly suggest the biological sex of the individual as female (Bass 1987).

Age determination for adults is far less reliable than for sub-adults. In estimating the age of the specimen we calculated the degree of ectocranial suture closure based on lateral-anterior and cranial vault sutures independently. In addition, we estimated mean age based on maxillary sutures of the palate region. Ectocranial vault suture closure suggested a mean age of 45.2 years with a standard deviation of 12.6 years providing a range of 31–65 years of age. Ectocranial lateral-interior suture closure estimates provided a mean age of 51.9 years (standard deviation of 12.5) suggesting an age range from 39–64 years old. Maxillary suture closure yielded an overall age range of 18–50 years. While suture closures vary considerably between individuals and are not always a reliable gauge indicator, these combined methods suggested an adult individual in her mid-40s to mid-50s (Zimmerman and Kelley 1982; Krogman and Iscan 1986).

Racial determination based on cranial remains can present numerous problems for the forensic anthropologist. The specimen had an overall cranial morphology that was small and rounded. The eye orbits were angular and the nasal spine sharp. The nasion was high and depressed with the nasal breath narrow. These series of craniofacial morphological patterns are fairly consistent with individuals of European ancestry (Paleopathology Association 1991).

Additional aspects of personal biology were also noted. No dentition was present with the cranium. However, all the anterior teeth including incisors and canines were present at death and lost subsequently since they exhibited sharp tooth sockets with no bone regeneration. All premolars and molars were lost during the individual's life as noted by bone redevelopment in the vacated tooth sockets. Examination revealed a cut and depression on the right parietal posterior to the coronal suture and immediately lateral to the sagittal suture, which runs anterior-to-posterior along the top of the skull. This slight depression showed signs of healing and could have been the result of the woman having her head hit by, or against, a hard object. However, it is highly unlikely that this trauma was severe enough to cause death.

Post-mortem trauma was apparent in a fresh fracture extending along the coronal plane from the right temporal to left temporal bones crossing the occipital posterior to the foramen magnum. This fracture consisting of a sharp cut exhibited no healing and may have been produced by the recent handling of the cranium by the suspects. Finally, and confusingly, coffin wear was noted in the area of the occipital protuberance (the back of the head where it would have lain on the bottom board of the coffin). Typically, this form of skeletal erosion occurs when the skull comes in contact with the wood of the coffin for an extended period of time – the wooden top board decays, collapses and presses against the forehead and the occipital where the head rests on the bottom board (Pokines and Baker 2013, 90–1). Evidently, the woman was laid in a traditional wooden coffin, but had never been buried in the ground.

In summary, our report to the police suggested that this specimen represented an adult, white female, probably 45–55 years of age and having sustained a minor impact to the upper left side of the skull. Cause of death and other pathological conditions were not discerned. And, most notably, the individual had probably died over 100 years ago, though she exhibited no signatures of ever having been buried underground (Bellantoni 1991a).

Upon identification of the adult female cranium, the Middletown Police requested further assistance in the investigation of a reported vandalism at a family mausoleum at Indian Hill Cemetery. Investigators had been working on the case for a couple of months and wanted to know if the Cromwell skull could have been taken from the Chauncey Family Tomb, a beautifully carved brownstone Romanesque memorial, which we first entered with the police in August, 1991 (Fig. 5.1). One investigative lead suggested that certain individuals with known occult associations might have broken into the mausoleum to remove skeletal remains for ritual purposes. To assist, we were asked to conduct further investigations inside the tomb to establish the identity of burials disturbed and determine if the woman's skull behind the car wash could had been stolen from this mausoleum (Bellantoni and Cooke 1997).

The practice of appropriating human skulls from old tombs for use in occult rituals has been recorded in a number of police cases around the country and widely reported in newspaper coverage due to their sensationalism (*Chicago Tribune* 2000; *Deseret News* 2000; Klepinger 2010, 229; *East Oregonian* 2014; Brown 2018; Ellis 2018, 103). Satanic occults, in particular, follow an annual cycle of ritual activities that require human skeletal remains at certain times of the year. A relatively trouble-free source of obtaining human skulls and other skeletal remains is the break-in of aged above-ground tombs – far easier than digging through 6 ft of hard-packed soil. Entry

Fig. 5.1. The Alsop-Chauncey-Mütter Mausoleum, Indian Hill Cemetery, Middletown, Connecticut (Photo: Brian Meyer).

can usually be easily achieved by severing through rusted doors and, once inside, rummaging through moldering coffins.

Law enforcement officials have long dealt with cemetery vandalisms associated with occult crimes. Overturning, breaking and/or stealing headstones is most common (Olson-Raymer 1989, 27), however, the digging up of graves and the entry into old tombs to obtain corpses or skeletons has also been a prevailing problem. The degree of cemetery desecration nationally is unknown, but in Connecticut I have been called into a least four potential occult cases in my 30-year tenure as State Archaeologist.

Although there are many types of occult activities, including witchcraft, voodoo, neo-paganism, wiccan, satanic, *Santeria* and *Palo Mayombe* (see Chapter 6) among others, it is the ritual components of Satanism and *Palo Mayombe* that have been the most directly implicated with the robbing of human skeletal remains from around the nation. Unfortunately, it is often difficult to implicate occultists in these types of crimes (Olsen-Raymer 1989, 27), though most law enforcement officials assume that true believers are the perpetrators of historical grave raiding. Human skulls, in particular, have been associated with cemetery vandalisms, as part of ritual altar offerings and in ceremonial caldrons. While the cranium behind the car wash was not found in the context of occult ceremony, ritual behavior was the leading hypothesis to explain the forced entry into the desecrated tomb at Indian Hill Cemetery.

****

Before the arrival of European settlers, the land that would become Middletown, Connecticut, was of course, occupied by Native Americans, namely the Wangunk Tribe, who called the area *Mattabeseck*. After the coming of Europeans to the Connecticut River Valley in the 1630s, Sowheag, the Wangunk sachem, built a fortification on a high, grassy hill located less than 2 miles (ca 3 km) west of the Connecticut River, which allowed considerable observation for great distances in all directions and could easily be defended against invaders. Upon this high peak, the Wangunks lived and conducted sacred ceremonies, which took on increased importance in response to drastic culture change and social upheaval generated by European contact. Wangunk populations decreased dramatically in the 17th century due to the introduction of smallpox and other Old World diseases, while English populations increased rapidly through continued migration to the New World. Indigenous Cultures, like the Wangunks, were stressed by intensified English colonialism and imperialism (Lavin 2017). The newly formed Connecticut Colony progressively appropriated Wangunk land, including the high hill, which would be transformed in the mid-19th century as a Euro-American place of burial.

Indian Hill Cemetery was dedicated in 1850 and represents the mid-19th-century concept of cemeteries as rural parks. With developing populations and the fear of epidemic diseases, a social movement was launched to remove cemeteries from crowded urban settings and create new graveyards in the immediate suburbs of the cities. This shift in burial locations was not only seen as hygienic, but also associated with the relatively new concept of death as peaceful repose. Hence, rural, park-like cemeteries in New England, starting with Mount Auburn in Cambridge, Massachusetts, in the 1830s were purposely designed and landscaped with exotic trees and shrubs, serene paths for walking and contemplation while commuting with the deceased (French 1974). This perception of cemeteries as public spaces was part of the City Beautiful Movement of the mid-19th century that encouraged an architectural and landscaping philosophy to promote prettified environments for public places (Weed 1912). Indian Hill Cemetery is an excellent example.

Indian Hill Cemetery was originally conceived by a group of prominent Middletown businessmen to replace the colonial era Mortimer Burying Ground on the city's Main Street. The original cemetery consisted of 20 acres/ca. 8 ha (it has since doubled in size), a portion of which is the site of the former Wangunk settlement, and is beautifully landscaped with several expensive and elegant monuments, including the Alsop-Chauncey-Mütter Mausoleum built in 1860 along the west-facing slope of the hill. Designed by Dr Horatio Stone, a prominent physician and sculptor (Beers 1884, 51), Indian Hill offered winding carriage paths circling up to the hill's prominence, where the Wangunks lived and conducted ceremonies. *No settlers' or modern graves have ever been interred on the top of the sacred hill in a rare sign of respect for the local Native culture* (DeFrance 2012, pers. comm.). Wangunk descendants are still part of the Middletown community (Lavin 2017) and have conducted contemporary ceremonies at the apex of Indian Hill.

Upon the cemetery's 1850 inaugural, Middletown residents that could afford to do so moved some of their deceased loved ones from other cemeteries to Indian Hill. Included were the graves of Richard (d. 1776) and Mary (d. 1829) Alsop and their family, who were relocated below-ground in front of the brownstone Alsop-Chauncey-Mütter

Mausoleum. Among other family members, Lucy Alsop Chauncey, who died in 1855 at the age of 56, would be reinterred inside the Chauncey Tomb.

****

A lifetime of experiences had already happened to Charles Chauncy (17th-century family spelling; Fig. 5.2) even before he immigrated to Plymouth, Massachusetts, in 1638. As a student at Westminster, he survived Guy Fawkes' gunpowder plot to blow up Parliament in 1605; he graduated from Trinity College, Cambridge, receiving his degree in Divinity in 1624 where he was appointed professor of Hebrew and Greek; four years later he became the Vicar of Ware, Hertfordshire, displeasing his Anglican superiors when he announced from the pulpit that there was a great "idolatry" within the church publicly revealing his staunch Puritan ideals. He was brought before the high courts in 1629 and again in 1634, when he opposed the erection of an altar rail between the ministers and the congregation. His ministry suspended, Rev. Chauncy was sentenced to imprisonment in 1635 and was not released for 2 years when his courage failed and he published a full "retraction" admitting his theological errors (something he would regret his entire life). Making matters worse, he further angered the Archbishop of Canterbury, Rev. William Laud, when he refused to read the Archbishop's book on *Lawful Sunday Sports* from the pulpit. Charles Chauncy, like the Rev. Peter Bulkeley (see Chapter 3) had little choice but abscond to New England (Fowler 1858).

Fig. 5.2. Charles Chauncy (1594-1672), Second President of Harvard College (Credit: Harvard University Archives).

Controversy continued to follow his ministry in Scituate, Massachusetts, where he resettled, after he advocated for baptism by complete submergence underwater, something even Puritans were reluctant to do in cold, wintry New England. Theological disagreements continued to frequent Rev. Chauncy, who always seemed to find a squabble with his colleagues (even over his paycheck), reaching a breaking point when he received an invitation to resume his pastorate back in Ware. Hence, in 1654, he set out for Boston ready to hop a ship back to England. However, immediately before he set sail, an invitation arrived requesting his services as the second president of Harvard College after the existing (and also controversial) president, Rev. Henry Dunster died. He readily accepted the position and the non-conformist minister would remain in New England for the rest of his life, giving rise to all Chauncey families in America (Fowler 1858).

When Charles Chauncy arrived in Plymouth, he already commanded a distinguished pedigree extending back on his father's side to Chauncy de Chauncy, who left the village of Chauncy near Amiens, France, and arrived in England with William the Conqueror in 1066. Through marriage, the Chauncy's claim their descent back to Charlemagne and Hildegard. Charles would marry Catherine Eyre, a descendant of old Wiltshire families who bore him seven children, six sons (all becoming ministers and graduates of Harvard) and one daughter, Sarah, who married Gershom Bulkelely (Chapter 3) in 1659 (Jacobus 1933).

Charles' grandson, Nathaniel, was the first graduate of Yale College, one of whose founders was his uncle Rev. Israel Chauncy, at their initial commencement held in 1702 at Saybrook, Connecticut (three other graduates had taken degrees elsewhere). He received a Bachelor of Arts and Master of Arts and became a celebrated New England minister in Durham, Connecticut. The family would see five consecutive generations of sons named Nathaniel, all of whom became prominent ministers and merchants (Fowler 1866).

The fifth Nathaniel Chauncey, born in 1758, was a tavern owner in Middletown, Connecticut. He married Abigail Olcott of Hartford on 20 April 1782 and together they would have eight children, the sixth of whom was a strapping boy they named Henry, whose immediate family would come to repose in the vandalized mausoleum in Indian Hill Cemetery.

Henry Chauncey was the patriarch of the Middletown family and a prominent merchant who had a business partnership with his father-in-law, Joseph Alsop. Alsop and Company maintained offices in Middletown, New York City and Valparaiso, Chile. Henry Chauncey would reside and represent the family's business interests in Chile for many years. His most notable achievement was becoming one of the founders of the Panamanian Railroad (Elliot 2014). In Colon, Panama, there is a commemorative carved bas-relief monument of him in profile.

****

On Tuesday, 3 September 1991, the State Archaeologist assisted by University of Connecticut anthropology students and volunteer avocational archaeologists from the Albert Morgan Archaeological Society, including Dave Cooke, re-entered the Chauncey Family Tomb to identify and interpret human remains and material culture as part of the crime scene investigation of the crypt's vandalism.

We were horrified by what we encountered. The family of Henry Chauncey occupied the center of the massive mausoleum between the Alsop and Mütter families. The entranceway is 20 ft high (6.10 m) and features brownstone-arched doorways leading to the 130 ft^2 (39.6 m^2) interior. Site investigation showed that four of the family vaults along the back wall had been violated. The marble tiled floor of the crypt was littered with disarticulated skeletal remains, shattered wooden and cast-iron coffins, burial clothing and linen. The desecrated vaults were that of Henry Chauncey, who died in 1863 at 68 years of age (Constitution 1863); Henry's wife, Lucy Alsop Chauncey, who died in 1855 at 56 years of age; and their grandsons, Richard Chauncey, whose birth and death were recorded on the same day, 26 January 1870, and Charles Chauncey, who died in Switzerland in 1873 aged 2 years, 6 months.

In order to facilitate the recording of the spatial distribution of human remains and coffin fragments scattered throughout crypt floor, a grid system was devised and constructed. Our crew built a frame consisting of wooden beams high enough to clear the piles of funerary materials on the floor. Fabrication of the frame was completed outside the mausoleum and a heavy twine was woven into 12 in (30 cm) grid squares. Upon completion, the frame was carried into the crypt and placed over the remains to facilitate horizontal and vertical recording. The grid was anchored to a datum point set in the north-west corner of the crypt's interior. The cemetery maintenance department furnished a gasoline-powered generator and several large floodlights for adequate illumination of the interior. Once in place, standard archaeological field methods were set to record the horizontal and vertical provenience as well as the orientation of the human remains and funerary artifacts, of the vandalized burials lying on the crypt floor. These procedures would help us develop a sequence of the transgressions.

Skeletal remains of the four desecrated individuals were recovered and sorted to develop a clear chain of criminal activity inside the tomb, as well as to create an inventory of elements represented throughout the tiled floor. In this process, we readily established that the cranium discovered behind the Cromwell car wash was that of Lucy Alsop Chauncey. Postcranial remains corresponded to her age, sex and post-decompositional breakdown and coloration of the bone noted in the earlier police report. In addition, Lucy's lower jaw was located during the tomb "excavation" and the mandibular condyles articulated precisely with the temporo-mandibular joint of the skull, providing positive identification. Lucy Chauncey's skeletal remains were rearticulated and eventually returned to her vandalized vault (Bellantoni 1993).

As a budding young archaeology student in the mid-1970s, I ferociously devoured all the books I could find on the lost ruins of past classical cultures. Rummaging through a used bookstore, I ran across a copy of John Lloyd Stephens' *Incidents of Travel in Central America, Chiapas and Yucatán, Vols I and II* and was mesmerized by his descriptions of rediscovered Mayan temples entangled within the dense Mesoamerican tropical forests. While Stephens' interpretations as to who built the ruins have been subsequently disproved, his 19th-century adventures into the lost cities of Central America read like an earlier version of the late 20th-century Indiana Jones movies (sans Nazis). While I never aspired to become a Mesoamerican archaeologist, I was thrilled to find a connection with John L. Stephens in one of my forensic cases. It turns out that Stephens was a close personal friend and business partner with Henry Chauncey, whom, along with William Aspinwall, founded the Panamanian railroad running between the Gulf of Mexico and the Pacific Ocean a half-century before the Panama Canal was constructed (Fig. 5.3).

The businessman in Henry Chauncey had serious doubts about the practicality of the Panamanian venture. He worried whether the investment of millions of dollars in capital needed for steamships and the formidable task of placing railroad tracks through the dense jungle and terrain of the Isthmus would return a profit. He saw the "rail-road project weighty and burdensome" (Elliot 2014, 47). Yet, Stephens had enough confidence and passion on behalf of the enterprise for the both of them, viewing the business as a "simple matter and easy of accomplishment." On a "stroll" along Broadway in the spring of 1849, Stephens convinced Chauncey of the venture with a detailed prognosis of the project: steamers navigating against the flow of the Chagres River on the Atlantic side, rail locomotives pulling upland toward the interior of the Continental spine, to the building of a horse-rail downhill to Panama City and the Pacific Ocean. The last leg of the journey would consist of waiting steamers set to ply the waters to San Francisco.

Fig. 5.3. John L. Stephens, William Aspinwall, Henry Chauncey, Panamanian Railroad Owners (Illustration from Harper's New Monthly Magazine, vol. 18, no. 103, January 1859).

All of this could be achieved for a mere investment of $3,000,000 inviting fortunes to be made for all (Stephens 1849; Elliot 2014, 47–48). Finally persuaded, Chauncey came onboard as a partner joining William Aspinwall in the enterprise. However, Stephens miscalculated his estimates and before completion the venture would cost in excess of $8,000,000 and a great sacrifice in human lives (Kemble 1943). Malaria, monsoons, tortuous swamps and cholera took its toll on engineers and manual laborers alike. Progress on the railroad was slow and laborious as men died and new workers were brought in – Irish, followed by Chinese, followed by Jamaicans. Chauncey's concerns seemed to be justified and Stephens' optimism challenged (McCullough 1977, 35).

Nonetheless, shortly after its completion, Stephens' enthusiasm would be validated. The Panamanian Railroad would become a huge financial success especially when gold was discovered in California. Enterprising Forty-Niners had three choices to reach the California goldfields: 1) they could travel on the Oregon/California Trial for 3–4 months crossing the continent by foot and wagon; 2) take a steamer rounding Cape

Horn circumnavigating the South American continent for 198 days; or, 3) if they could afford the costs of steamships and railroad, make the trip from New York to San Francisco via Panama in a week! Many chose to do so and with the government contract to carry United States mail between the coasts, fortunes would be made.

However, neither Stephens or Chauncey would live long enough to witness the full financial success of the railroad. John L. Stephens was found unconscious under a ceiba tree in Panama and rushed to New York City where he would lapse into a coma and die on 13 October 1852. Eleven years later, Henry Chauncey expired suddenly at a friend's residence in Mount Holly, New Jersey, in 1863 aged 68 (Elliot 2014, 52). Due to his unexpected death, an autopsy was performed before his body was transported to New York City for funeral services, and, from there, on to Middletown for final burial in the recently completed family mausoleum at Indian Hill Cemetery. In a fitting tribute to one of the founders of the Panamanian Railroad, the SS *Henry Chauncey*, a two-mast, side-paddle steamer, was launched in October 1864, shortly after his death, serving the Pacific Mail Steamship Company and transporting postal and passengers between New York City and Panama (Fig. 5.4). The steamship remained on this route until 1869 and was later used as a transport vessel between New York and Jamaica. It burned at sea on 16 August 1871 off the Carolina Coast with no loss of life (Chandler and Potash 2007).

Henry and Lucy's children would inherit a great fortune. However, due to the development of the transcontinental railroad in 1869 and its ability to connect the East

Fig. 5.4. The SS Henry Chauncey *(Credit: Courtesy of the California History Room, California State Library, Sacramento, California).*

and West coasts of the United States in just 4 days, the Panamanian Railroad became obsolete. Coupled with fiscal mismanagement by their heirs, the family fortune was all but lost (Elliot 2014, 68).

****

Based on forensic and archaeological investigations, we proposed the following sequence of events for the criminal activities within the Chauncey Tomb: Upon entry into the crypt, achieved by snapping the padlock with a large cutters, the vandals' initial act of desecration appears to have been conducted on the burials of the two children in the extreme lower left vault of the back wall (Figs 5.5 and 5.6): Richard Alsop Chauncey, who died on the day of his birth in 1870, and Charles Chauncey, who passed away in Chexbris, Switzerland, aged 2 years, 6 months in 1873. Both children were the grandsons of Henry and Lucy Chauncey. The vandals apparently pried off the marble slab bearing the children's epitaphs with a crowbar since scar marks are discernible on the upper left-hand corner of the marble slab, dropping it in one piece face down on the tile floor exposing two small coffins housed side-to-side in the vault. The vandals removed the coffins and placed them on the tiled floor on top of the displaced marble slab in front of their vaults (Bellantoni 1991b).

The remains of the infant, Richard Chauncey, had been placed in a small wooden coffin and were almost totally decomposed; however, Charles Chauncey had been wrapped carefully and encased within a zinc liner, which was then placed within a traditional wooden coffin for oceanic transportation from Switzerland to Middletown. This child's skeletal remains were well preserved. The vandals proceeded to remove the liner from the coffin discarding the latter along the left wall. Unaware of the

Fig. 5.5. Burial vaults on the interior back wall of the Chauncey Tomb. Lower left shows the coffins of two children. Upper right is Henry Chauncey's cast-iron coffin replaced after the investigation (Credit: Middletown Police Department).

Fig. 5.6. Interior of the Chauncey Tomb floor after vandalism, Note marble epitaph stone, skeletal remains, wooden coffin fragments and funerary clothing (Credit: Middletown Police Department).

Fig. 5.7. Lower limb skeletal elements, boot (center right) of Charles Chauncey (2.5 years of age) thrust aside on the marble-tiled floor of Chauncey mausoleum (Credit: Middletown Police Department).

orientation of the skull, the vandal's punched holes on opposite sides of the liner apparently to remove its cranial contents.

Charles Alsop Chauncey was dressed in a lace baptismal robe with black high-top buckle shoes. At the outset, the criminals broke into the base of the coffin and removed the foot, still embedded in its shoe. When they attempted to extract the foot, the entire right leg was detached at the hip. We located the leg at the extreme right side of the crypt 15 ft (4.57 m) from its coffin, having been tossed across the floor apparently in disgust. Unsatisfied, they punctured a second hole through the zinc liner at the head region of the coffin and removed what remained of the skull. However, the cranium of the 2-year old child was in numerous fragments due to the lack of fusion of the bones at that early age. The cranial vault plates were then discarded to the left of the coffin liner and strewn on the marble slab between the wood and the zinc liner (Fig. 5.7). The entire right booted leg with foot embedded and the pieces of the cranium were the only skeletal elements of Charles Chauncey detached from his small coffin.

The vandals next proceeded to desecrate the vault of Henry and Lucy Alsop Chauncey, located in the center of the crypt, second row. Once again, they removed the marble tombstone by prying the upper left-hand corner with a crowbar, similar to opening the children's vault. However, this stone evidently proved difficult to dislodge. To free the slab, they smashed it with the bar hammer or similar tool. The stone shattered from the impact of the blows, which were delivered to the center of the tombstone, sending marble fragments tumbling to the floor except for a large portion of its right side that still remained hinged on the wall. This piece bore Lucy Chauncey's epitaph and remained on the vault wall, though forced out of the way to gain entry to her remains.

From the analysis of the human remains strewn on the crypt floor it appears that Lucy Chauncey was removed from her vault first. Her remains had been lying in a desiccated hardwood coffin with a glass viewing plate on the lid. The interior of the coffin was lined with delicate linen and she was dressed in a tasteful blouse with ribbons. When vandals attempted to slide the desiccated coffin out of the vault housing, it literally exploded in their hands, crumbling, and along with the skeletal remains of Mrs. Chauncey plummeting to the floor. The distribution of skeletal and fragmented wooden coffin remains from Lucy's burial were scattered at the base of the wall directly under her vault (Fig. 5.8). Disposed skeletal elements consist of all

Fig. 5.8. The inferior portion of Lucy Chauncey's wooden coffin showing skeletal elements of the lower limbs within her burial vault (Credit: Middletown Police Department).

Fig. 5.9. Cast-iron coffin and autopsied skull plate of Henry Chauncey as found inside the Chauncey Tomb (Credit: Middletown Police Department).

upper body postcranial remains above the sacrum, while all elements of the pelvic girdle and lower limbs remained *in situ* within the vault. Hence, only the upper portions of Lucy Chauncey's body had been drawn out of the vault and strewn onto the floor. The skeletal element conspicuously missing from the floor is the cranium, which appears to have been the only bone removed from the interior of the crypt. A brass earring wore by Lucy was found among the floor debris.

After the destruction of Mrs Chauncey's coffin, the vandals appear to have turned their attention to the heavy cast-iron coffin housing the remains of her husband, Henry. Cast-iron caskets were beginning to be manufactured in the early 1860s and their appearance attests to the high socio-economic status of the Chauncey family. Henry's coffin had a shield-shaped glass window for viewing the face during the funeral service with a metal cover that bolted over the window and fitted for final burial afterward. A silver-coated name plate was located and inscribed:

Henry Chauncey
Died 28 Apr. 1863
Aged 68 years

The vandals slid the iron coffin out of the vault, crashing it to the floor, where they attempted to pry it open, but the rusted metal prohibited entry, so it appears that they then turned the coffin over and deliberately smashed the thin rusted metal bottom of the casket, which evidently broke apart easily (Fig. 5.9). Mr. Chauncey was clothed in a formal three-piece suit that was badly decomposed. The suit consisted of pants, vest and a formal jacket with long tails with the bones of the arms and legs still embedded in the sleeves and pants of the burial suit. Interestingly, we recovered a set of vulcanized rubber dentures tinted pink to simulate gums with porcelain-bonded teeth snugly tailoring his lower jaw (Fig. 5.10). Evidentially, Henry had lost his entire mandibular tooth row and when vulcanite dentures became available in the 1850s,

Fig. 5.10. Lower volcanized rubber dentures fitting the mandible of Henry Chauncey (Photo: Author).

he had a set molded to fit his lower jaw. We found no evidence of upper tooth row dentures. Henry's remains were dispersed throughout the crypt floor and overlaid the remains of both Lucy and Charles Chauncey.

The skull of Mr Chauncey was in two pieces. The cranial vault had been hand-sawed transversely as a result of the autopsy at the time of his death. The craniofacial complex appears to have been crushed in the act of vandalism and could not be reconstructed. As a result of the autopsy procedure, two corroded metal stains were located on the right and left temporal bones inferior to the squamous suture. The metal discolorations probably represented double-pointed carpet tacks used to fasten the calvaria together after the autopsy was completed, the brain having been removed during the original forensic examination. The metal fasteners would have kept the transected cranium together during transportation to his funeral in New York City and ultimate burial in Middletown.

In summary, the distribution of skeletal and coffin remains on the crypt floor suggests a sequence of vandalism commencing with the children's vaults on the bottom row. Mrs Chauncey was desecrated immediately afterward and, finally, Henry Chauncey's remains overlay the remains of his wife and grandchildren. Left undisturbed in the mausoleum were the burials of Frederick Chauncey, Henry and Lucy's son, and his immediate family, whose remains reposed along the top row of vaults, much harder for the criminals to access easily from the floor level (Bellantoni 1991b).

The motive for the defacement appears to be the obtaining of human skulls for possible occult rituals. Burglary for grave goods seems unlikely for a number of reasons: 1) Instead of simply punching circular holes into Charles Chauncey's zinc-lined coffin, the pilfers would have attempted to open the entire box to search for jewelry or other valuables; 2) the lower half of Lucy Chauncey's coffin would not have been left in the vault but rather it would have been thoroughly inspected and her earrings would not have been missed; 3) artifacts were left behind in Henry Chauncey's coffin, some of which could have monetary value; and 4) the remains of all individuals would not have been so haphazardly scattered. There is no sign of systematic search for artifacts that one would expect if the vandals were looking for memorabilia to sell or collect.

All other materials in the crypt were related to various elements of coffin architecture. While negative evidence can never be used in archaeological analysis, that is, we cannot account for what may have been taken and thus not recovered, we do know that Lucy Chauncey's cranium was the only complete skull of the four burials vandalized and the one item retrieved by the police that we can testify was removed from the tomb.

Partially based on the forensic archaeology conducted at the Chauncey Tomb, Middletown police arrested a male suspect involved with numerous crimes including the armed robbery of more than 65 firearms from a local gun store the previous year (Kranold 1992). The suspect was taken into custody in lieu of $10,000 bond following his arrest and arraignment on four counts of interfering with a cemetery or grave site, one count each of 1st-degree burglary and 1st-degree criminal mischief and 6th-degree larceny. When police entered his residence with a search warrant, they found satanic paraphernalia, some arranged on a makeshift altar and painted on the walls were the numerals "666", the numeral of the Beast, or the devil's number. The suspect pleaded not guilty, claiming the skull belonged to his girlfriend and he had no knowledge of how she obtained it (Petry 1992).

So, why was Lucy Chauncey's cranium disposed of behind a car wash and not kept for future occult rituals? Well, we do not know for sure, but the police were closing in on the suspect for the previous burglary investigations and it could be that he felt pressure to dispose of the human skull before the police found it in his possession when they executed the anticipated search warrant.

Forensic archaeology and anthropology continue to play an important role in the efforts to collect physical evidence from crime scenes whenever human skeletal remains are involved. Archaeological field techniques have been designed to obtain the most information from a given site even when at times very little cultural material remains for analysis. The application of these field techniques in a criminal investigation will, hopefully, result in a greater degree of accuracy in the location of physical evidence and the best insurance for the recovery of material remains that may otherwise be lost. In this case, it led to the conviction of the vandal. The Chauncey tomb, we hope, is an example of this cooperative working relationship.

Chapter 6

Edwin Denison Morgan Tomb

Trembling, across the plain my course I held.
And found the grave-yard, loitering through the gloom.
And, in the midst, a hell-red, wandering light.
Walking in fiery circles round the tomb.

Philip Freneau, *The Houses of the Night*

"And ...!" the young woman brusquely shouted as her abusive boyfriend was being ushered out of the apartment by two policemen, "He has human skulls in the closet!" The revelation stopped Detective David Rohon of the New Britain Police Department in his tracks. Rohon had been called to the apartment to investigate a domestic dispute between a young Hispanic couple and was taking the man into custody hoping to resolve their altercation when the woman's cry caused the detective to make an about-face.

A carry-on suitcase was rolled out of a bedroom closet and opened, exposing a human skull and several postcranial skeletal remains. A decorative, three-legged terracotta pot with wooden sticks sticking out of the top and dried blood on the rim contained a second human skull (Fig. 6.1). Detective Rohon's immediate concern was homicide.

Under interrogation at the police station, the suspect admitted to possession of these human skeletal remains explaining that they were used in Santeria religion, of which he was a priest. However, he assured the police that he was a priest of the "good side" and that he did not practice the "dark side," or Palo Mayombe sect of the religion, which required human bones for their ceremonies (Gill *et al.* 2009). He was storing the remains for a Dada, or high priest, of the Palo Mayombe to be used in an upcoming healing ritual. The man further acknowledged that he went with this same high priest to Black Rock State Park in Watertown, Connecticut to recover some rocks and soil for use during the rituals, but he insisted that he had not procured the bones. The Dada, young man revealed, had paid accomplices to remove skeletons from old cemeteries to gain extra energy for the healing process (Rathbun 2013, 1). The high priest especially desired bones stolen from someone who was influential in life, as their remains possessed the most power in death, giving the healing ceremony extra potency.

Fig. 6.1. Clay Palo Mayombe pot with 20 sticks protruding around the rim (Photo: Molly Rathbun).

The next day (11 April 2008), Det. Rohon transferred the luggage and clay vessel to the Office of the State's Chief Medical Examiner, where Dr H. Wayne Carver II, assigned a case number (ME 08-13785), verified that the skeletons were human and listed the cause of death as "Historical Remains" since the bones exhibited cortical exfoliation and a dry, brittle texture indicative of individuals long deceased. Professor Gerald (Jerry) Conlogue, diagnostic imaging researcher at Quinnipiac University, who also works with the Medical Examiner's Office, x-rayed the skull and all of the long bones in the suitcase and used plane radiography and computed tomography (CT) to image the clay pot, revealing details of the embedded skull, while also detecting images of two horseshoes and various bird bones among many other items. Searching through the suitcase, investigators found a metal nameplate that read, *Mary B.P. Morgan 1857-1886*, along with two pieces of clothing. Mary Catherine Sonntag, specialized photographer for the Medical Examiner's

Office, immediately began searching for photographs and genealogical information on Mary B.P. Morgan.

Coincidentally, the Hartford Police Department was conducting an investigation into a tomb break-in at Cedar Hill Cemetery in the city's South End that had been desecrated a few weeks before the New Britain arrest. The vandalized mausoleum was built in 1883 by Edwin Denison Morgan (1811–1883), a Major General of Volunteers in the Union Army during the Civil War and a former New York Governor and Senator, as a place of repose for his family. Combining the two investigations, the State Archaeologist was invited to join the team to excavate the contents of the ceremonial pot and to further investigate the tomb.

****

Honorary pallbearers following behind the coffin of Edwin Denison Morgan (Fig. 6.2) were a "Who's Who" of late 19th-century American politics and business, including former United States President Ulysses S. Grant, and the current President, Chester A. Arthur. Business tycoons, such as John Jacob Astor, who would perish aboard the *Titanic*, and J. Pierpont Morgan, a distant cousin and arguably the wealthiest man in the country, were also recruited as pallbearers. Immediate family members attending the funeral at the Brick Presbyterian Church on New York City's Fifth Avenue included among others, Edwin's widow, Eliza, his grandson Edwin III and his wife Mary B.P. Morgan. First cousin, Morgan Gardner Bulkeley (see Chapter 3), then Mayor of Hartford, Connecticut also marched with the family behind the casket (Anon. 1883).

The funeral procession did not have far to walk. Morgan's mansion at 411 Fifth Avenue (Fig. 6.3), where he died from heart failure on 14 February 1888 (Valentine's Day) at 72 years of age and where he was waked, resided directly across the street from the Brick Church, which was filled to capacity with friends, acquaintances and dignitaries. An overflow crowd of thousands stood silently in wintry, drizzling rain as Morgan's coffin slowly traversed Fifth Avenue. While many endured the cold under black umbrellas to pay their last respects to the noted politician and businessman, many had come to catch a glimpse of

Fig. 6.2. Edwin Denison Morgan (1811–1883) (Credit: Brady-Handy Photograph Collection, Library of Congress).

Fig. 6.3. Back side of Edwin Denison Morgan's Fifth Avenue Mansion and garden viewed from 37th Street. The steeple of the Brick Presbyterian Church can be seen left (Credit: Old Buildings of New York City, New York: Brentano's, 1907).

President Arthur, General Grant and other celebrities in attendance. The funeral was a major event in a major city, fully reflecting Edwin Denison Morgan's influence and prestige (Miller 2013).

He was said to have achieved more in his lifetime than any other "Morgan" had ever since the days of Elizabethan England, and that's quite a statement considering Edwin Denison came from such a distinguished and extended pedigree (Morgan 1902, 121). The name "Mor-gan" means "by the sea" or "son of the sea." Legend has it that King Arthur's youngest son was born in Glamorgan, South Wales and named "Mor-gan" – man born by the sea. Morgan's ancestors served Henry V and other English monarchs in many and varying capacities before their various lines came to America in the 17th century (Morgan 1902, 5).

Edwin D. Morgan was a direct descendant of James Morgan (1607–1685), genealogically recognized today as an appendage of the "Morgan-Avery" lines. James sailed from Bristol, England, on the ship, *Mary* in 1636 landing at Boston in Massachusetts Bay. He first settled to the north at Sandy Bay, near Gloucester on Cape Ann, but found the rocky coast miserably uncomfortable and filled with unrests from local Native American tribes. So he ventured south to Roxbury where he met and married Margery Hill in 1640 (Morgan 1902, 102).

With a young family in hand, James moved further south to New London, Connecticut in 1649, where he would hold offices with both the town and church. The family prospered and by 1662 James was listed as the third highest taxpayer in the developing city. His son John (b. 1645) became Deputy to the General Court from New London (Morgan 1902, 106). John (2)'s second wife, Elizabeth Williams, was the granddaughter of Governor Theophilus Eaton, a co-founder of the New Haven Colony. John and Elizabeth's second born (John would sire a total of 16 children by two marriages), William (#10 overall), married Mary Avery in July 1716, hence linking the Morgan and Avery lines. William's son, William (2), married another Avery (his cousin) and had ten children, including William (3), who enlisted at the Lexington alarm and served as a sergeant under General Israel Putnam at the Battle of Bunker Hill on 17 June 1775. Of William (3)'s 17 children and their descendants, many would go on to prominence in American history, most notably his grandson, Edwin Denison Morgan (Morgan 1902, 118–19).

Edwin was born in Washington, Berkshire County, Massachusetts, to Deacon Jasper Morgan and Catherine Avery (yet another cousin marriage), on 8 February 1811. When Edwin was 13 years old, the family moved to Windsor, Connecticut, where his father operated a farm. In 1826, at the age of 16, Edwin attended Bacon Academy in Colchester (see Chapter 3) for one term where he showed an aptitude for mathematics, though that one semester represented his sole formal education. Two years later, he joined his Uncle Nathan (his father's younger brother) in a wholesale grocery business in Hartford and within 3 years became a full partner. Edwin had a great capacity for self-development that followed him throughout his life. After serving on the Common Council of Hartford, Edwin moved to New York City in 1836 and began business there as a merchant co-establishing the E.D. Morgan & Company import house (Morgan 1902, 120).

New York City is where Edwin flourished as a merchant, banker and financier. Before long his commercial enterprises extended throughout the United States and into parts of Europe. Edwin's political career also jumpstarted there in 1849 when he was appointed to the City Council's Board of Aldermen and was elected to the New York State Senate all in the same year. Formerly a zealous member of the Whig Party, he switched when the Republican Party emerged due to his strong opposition to slavery. Edwin made an immediate impression and was selected as Vice-President of the first National Republican convention held at Pittsburgh, Pennsylvania, which nominated John C. Frémont for the Presidency. The budding politician advanced to the chairmanship of the National Republican Committee, a position he would hold until 1864 and once again from 1872–1876. He was overwhelmingly elected Governor of the State of New York for two terms starting in 1858 and occupied the chairmanship of the Republican convention in 1860 that would nominate Abraham Lincoln as President (Rawley 1968).

When the American Civil War broke out in 1861, Edwin Denison Morgan earned a reputation as the "Great War Governor" after he recruited over 125,000 soldiers from all over New York to serve on the front lines of the Union Army. Out of gratitude, Lincoln awarded him a commission as Major General of Volunteers, a title he appreciatively consented to, but only on the condition that he would not receive a salary, which endeared him to his President and the Country. During the war (1863), he was elected to the United States Senate representing the State of New York, serving on Committees of Commerce, Manufacturing, and Finance among others, and functioning in that capacity until 1869, when he finally retired from public office. Twice, he was offered the cabinet position of Secretary of the Treasury, once by Lincoln and then later by his friend, Chester A. Arthur. He declined both appointments, much to the regret of both presidents (Morgan 1902, 120; Sobel and Raimo 1978).

At the time of his death and the elaborate Fifth Avenue funeral, Edwin Denison Morgan had retired from politics but kept occupied running his extensive commercial and financial undertakings. He had served both his State and Nation in a most practical and thorough business manner. He never stooped to political shenanigans and haranguing, but rather seldom spoke or debated during Senate meetings, though when he did speak up, his fellow senators listened attentively to his counsel. In his obituary, the New York Times characterized Edwin as "possessed of an iron constitution, with unbounded energy and industry, and with a rare precision of purpose as well as capacity for systematic labor ... and [he] was always listened to with respect" (*New York Times*, 1883). The Reverend Henry J. Van Dyke, Jr., eulogized Edwin Denison Morgan as a "strong man ... an honest man ... a good man ... a Christian man" (Anon. 1883, 41–62)

That was the public side of Edwin's illustrious career. His private life was also eventful, but, at times, filled with much heartbreak. He married Eliza Matilda Waterman in 1833 and together they gave birth to five children, four of which died dreadfully young: Frederick Avery Morgan at 3 years of age, Gilbert Henry Morgan, within weeks of his birth, and both Caroline Matilda Morgan and Alfred Waterman Morgan in their initial year of life. Edwin and Eliza's firstborn son, Edwin Denison Morgan, Jr, was the lone surviving offspring into adulthood but he too died prematurely at the age of 45, though living long enough to marry (Sarah Elizabeth Archer) and have one child, Edwin Denison Morgan III, whose first wife was Mary Brewer Penniman Morgan. All of them would be buried at the family plot in Cedar Hill Cemetery, Hartford, Connecticut (Fig. 6.4).

****

At the time of the Morgan Tomb investigation, the Chauncey Mausoleum (see Chapter 5), Indian Hill Cemetery, Middletown, Connecticut had been the largest burial chamber we had ever entered. However, that burial chamber contained the remains of three families (Alsop, Chauncey and Mütter), while the Edwin Denison Morgan

Fig. 6.4. Westside view of the Edwin Morgan Tomb, Cedar Hill Cemetery, Hartford, Connecticut. Note headstones of Morgan family buried outside the tomb (Photo: Brian Meyer).

Tomb, Cedar Hill Cemetery, Hartford was as large but constructed to house only the remains of Morgan's immediate family and their descendants.

Designed by the prominent architect Stanford White (1853–1906), who was the architect for the original Madison Square Garden in New York City, the Morgan Tomb was constructed as a massive "two-tiered solid granite ashlar building with buttress-like supports at the corners and a flanking entrance, stepped cornice line and low pyramidal roof with bulky rounded finials above four central triangular gables" (Ransom 1996). Sets of windows adorn three sides of the mausoleum permitting light to penetrate the interior ground-level floor. The tomb's entrance faces east toward the rising sun. Originally, two sculptures by noted New York artist Augustus Saint-Gaudens (1848–1907) were to have been placed on either side of the tomb's entrance, but these were destroyed by fire at Cedar Hill Cemetery before their completion. Nonetheless, the work enjoyed a "considerable reputation" (Dryfhout 2008, 136) and models of these sculptures would eventually become part of the fireplace mantelpiece for Cornelius Vanderbilt's Fifth Avenue mansion and are today part of the collections of the Metropolitan Museum of Art in New York City (Dimmick 1999, 272).

The tomb appears as formidable as a fortress and resides on the apex of a north–south glacial drumlin referred to as Hill House Ridge (Section 12, Lot 6) of Cedar Hill Cemetery. While all of Edwin's descendants are interred at the grand tomb, ten individuals are buried in separate below ground graves outside the west or back of the tomb structure, while nine members of his nuclear family and his daughter-in-law repose inside the mausoleum.

On 15 November 2013, the State Archaeologist accompanied by students and faculty from Quinnipiac University, including Jerry Conlogue and Dr Jaime Ullinger, a bioanthropologist, and University of Connecticut students, entered the Morgan Tomb to assess damage associated with the vandalism and conduct an inventory of human skeletal remains to be compared with those discovered during the New Britain arrest. Under the direction of Bill Griswold, superintendent of Cedar Hill Cemetery, ground crews unlocked the padded, metal door leading into the two-tiered mausoleum for our team to enter.

Descending steep stone steps to the lower crypt area, we encountered two fragmented marble slabs with engraved epitaphs and brass handles leaning against the left wall at the base of the stairway. The marble pieces had been shattered and pulled off the wall to gain entry into the individual vaults, similar to those encountered in the Chauncey Tomb. Where the epitaphs were torn off the walls, two caskets were exposed in their original placements. The two marble slabs, 7 ft (2.13 m) in length when reconstructed, verified the names of "Edwin Denison Morgan" and "Mary B.P. Morgan", the occupants of the desecrated vaults.

Reminiscent of the Chauncey Tomb, individual burials were placed into vaults shelved on walls, one directly ahead as you enter and the other to the right, which housed a single burial surrounded by five unused vaults. Coffins were laid parallel to the walls so that the sides of the coffins faced outward, unlike the Chauncey Tomb where the coffins rest perpendicular into the wall, feet first toward the back of the tomb (Fig. 6.5). The floor was expensively tiled with marble and the walls around the crypts were bricked in red and yellow colors (Fig. 6.6). The upper or ground level of the mausoleum contained an extensive foyer where sunlight streamed through three sets of windows onto an area designed for private meditation.

Inspecting the interior desecrated area my initial impression was that the vandalized tomb was unusually tidy. Similar to clandestine activities at the Chauncey Tomb, coffins had been removed from their individual vaults, dropped to the floor, shattered to gain entry and rummaged through, but the floor was not littered with human remains, wooden and metal caskets or other debris as we had observed in Middletown. When I shared my thoughts about the overall neatness of the chamber after such despicable vandalism, the cemetery workers acknowledged that when the Hartford Police first investigated the break in, they replaced the coffins into their appropriate vaults and leaned the shattered coffin lids against the wall, restoring order to the violated tomb. Orderly, but, in the same way, Christian burials had been desecrated for purposes of non-Christian rituals.

Examining the contents of the two disturbed caskets, we composed an inventory of human skeletal remains still contained within to compare with the inventory of remains pilfered and retained at the Medical Examiner's Office. For example, while most of the

Fig. 6.5. Exposed cast-iron coffin (Burial 1652) of Edwin Denison Morgan in his burial vault (Photo: Molly Rathbun).

Fig. 6.6. Exposed wooden coffin (Burial 1314) of Mary B.P. Morgan in her burial vault (Photo: Molly Rathbun).

skeletal elements of Edwin Denison Morgan, including the skull, some vertebrae and ribs, were removed during the vandalism, the left tibia and fibula were found in their anatomical positions at the foot end of his coffin. Missing elements corresponded to skeletal remains found in the luggage (Case No. 08-04930) and clay pot, however, we could not account for all of Edwin's long bones suggesting that more skeletal elements were removed from the tomb than were recovered from the New Britain apartment. On the other hand, between the contents of the coffin and suitcase we could reconstruct the complete skeleton of Mary B.P. Morgan.

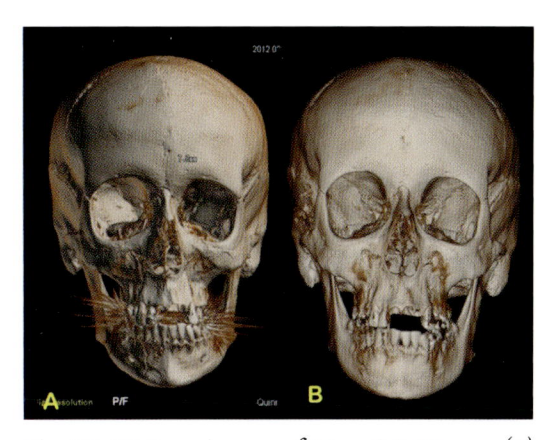

Fig. 6.7. CT Scan images of Mary B.P. Morgan (A) and Edwin Denison Morgan (B). Note that the streaks in the left image radiating from gold dental fillings (Credit: Bioanthropology Research Institute, Quinnipiac University).

The coloration and wear on the bones matched the remains from the luggage and clay pot to those in the tomb, as did the forensic aspects of the skeletons fit biological characteristics of the patriarch and his daughter-in-law. Mary's cranium was gracile with sharp supraorbital margins and open sutures consistent with a young female. She had a complete set of dentition, though the upper anterior teeth had come loose after death, and three cavities of her mandibular molars displayed gold-fillings (Fig. 6.7, A). The skull embedded within the ritual vessel corresponded to expectations of an older adult, Caucasian male: the overall architecture of the cranium is robust with large mastoid processes and completely closed cranial sutures, the nasal breadth is narrow, and the nasal bone is relatively long. Like Mary, Edwin also had gold fillings signifying that the family had the financial resources for consistent dental care (Fig. 6.7, B). Skulls, especially, along with assorted long bones appear to have been the main targets of the vandalism.

****

The Dada chanted invocations in a language unfamiliar to the patient as he placed the skull of Edwin Denison Morgan into the decorative clay vessel. He danced and positioned animal and manufactured objects as offerings into the cauldron, each artifact characteristic of deities possessing specific spiritual powers affecting social or physical health. An ignited red candle was placed at the bottom of the pot permitting smoke to emit through orifices of the robust skull. Orisha, dynamic spirits, are believed to play an important role in the overall health of the individual by releasing *Aché*, a powerful energy that connects humans and spirits to the Earth. If the high priest performs the ritual appropriately, the patient will be spiritually and physically healed of illnesses.

Orisha (Lucumi) is the primary faith of Santeria ("Way of the Saints") and along with Palo Mayombe stem from African-Caribbean religious traditions. When West African captives from the Yoruba region were brought by force to Cuba in the 16th century to work sugar plantations, they were exposed to their slaveholder's Catholicism (Brandon 2012). With forced conversion and, in order to preserve their traditional African beliefs, they fused elements of Christianity with Santeria creating a syncretic religion that was soon outlawed by the Spanish government. Enslaved Yoruba peoples found commonalities between their deities and the concept of Catholic *santos* (saints) and infused both elements into their Native rituals. In actuality, many practitioners continued their primary faith as a means of surviving the horrors of captivity by disguising Santeria with elements of Christianity, which were retained when Caribbean immigrants came to the United States (Kosmin *et al.* 2001).

In the early 1960s, Cuban migrations expanded into Miami, Dade County, Florida, due to the island nation's takeover by the communist regime of Fidel Castro, and with them came major influences of Santeria and Palo religions. Subsequently, the practices spread to Latino communities across the country as Cubans sought work opportunities in industrial urban centers like New Britain and Hartford, Connecticut. The Mariel Boatlift of 1980 transported a new wave of Cuban refugees, many of whom, unfortunately, were criminals as Castro emptied out his prisons to rid himself of internal problems by sending unwanted convicts to the United States. Though all the refugees professed to being Christians, some adhered to the modified beliefs of Santeria and Palo.

Palo Mayombe developed in a similar pattern as Santeria. The word *Palo* (*Las Reglas de Congo*), or "stick" in Spanish, is derived from the use of wooden sticks within their ceremonies. Palo belief system originated in the Congo basin of Central Africa among Bantu speakers (Kail 2008, 72), whose worship incorporates receptacles that contain sticks, animals, earth, wax, feathers, mercury, metal objects and human remains as symbols to manipulate the Aché spirits to foster a successful outcome for the patient's wellbeing or, in some cases, to cause possible harm. Hence, its reference as the "dark side."

While Santeria and Palo faiths developed along similar trajectories within the African diaspora and are interrelated, they often incorporate distinct rituals and maintain separate styles of healing and worship (Winburn *et al.* 2016, 3). Though similarities include dancing, singing and drumming to attract the spirit world, Santeria involves the engagement of Orishas, who are beseeched to guide the human patient seeking the life forces that the spirits contain. It is considered a benign cult of the deities (Kail 2008, 72), while Palo has been described as a "cult of the dead" (Winburn *et al.* 2016, 4), where priests engage the deceased through skeletal remains, to transform the destinies of the living (Ochoa 2004, 245), whether it be to heal or to cause harm. The more successful the departed were in life, the more spiritual energy and intensity their bones possess in death guaranteeing the desired ritualistic outcomes. Santeria ceremonial objects are usually displayed for all to see, while Palo objects are left secreted, often hidden in a shed or closet (Olson-Raymer 1989, 48; Windburn *et al.* 2016, 4). Santeria rituals do not include human remains; Palo always do.

The pot or cauldron represents the "essence of *Palo*" (Bettelheim, 2001, 36). Within each pot is created an assemblage of objects, animate and inanimate, with differing symbolic expressions and values, synchronized to express varying emotions. For example, the blood of animal sacrifices stirs the soul, while feathers quiet it (Ochoa 2004). Stones are sacred with special powers (Olson-Raymer 1989, 48). And, always, there is the dead one, represented in tangible human remains (Ochoa 2004), providing the potent force to enliven the Aché working in harmony to perform their supernatural activity. The metaphysical belief is that "dead ones" do their work even more efficiently if the remains have been stolen from a grave (Cabrera 1983) and are of individuals who achieved a high level of socio-economic status in life. Stealing the soul of the powerful to help the weak can be interpreted as the cultural shaping of the institution of captivity, the metaphorical relationship between the slaver and the enslaved.

As we were appalled at the disarray of human skeletal remains and coffin materials strewn upon the floor of the Chauncey Tomb by the occult vandals, we were equally as horrified at the desecration of the two burials at the Morgan Tomb. In both cases, the disruption of Christian burials for the purposes of non-Christian ritual was equally as atrocious. The disruption of the dead and the secretive placement of human remains in suitcases and ceremonial vessels were difficult to fathom.

****

Reconvening at the Medical Examiner's Office, our research team gathered to systematically remove the contents of the decorated ceramic pot. Jerry Conlogue and the team from Quinnipiac University's Bioanthropology Research Institute, Department of Diagnostic Imaging had conducted CT-scans of the vessel prior to the removal of any objects and human remains (Figs 6.8 and 6.9). Transverse sections of the pot established the skull amid a host of ritualistic objects, including horseshoes, animal and mineral remains.

While there were no symbols etched or painted on the vessel, it did exhibit two carved motifs around the rim and central body. There were 20 sharpened sticks protruding out the top and positioned around the outer rim surrounding the human cranium, which had been placed down into the middle of the pot. Interspersing the sticks were seven large white bird feathers as well as smaller ones lying flat on top of the cranial vault. The sticks were removed individually, inventoried and examined. All were honed to a sharp point on the protruding end and left blunt on the end embedded into the pot. Many of the sticks had numbers written toward the unsharpened end ranging from 1 to 21; however, some numbers were not represented and others appeared more than once, while three were totally illegible. The number sequence was as follows: 1 and 3 appear twice, 4, 6/9, 7, 8, 10, 11, 16, 17, 19, 20 and 21. There were seven sticks without numbers, but with blue, white and/or red marks painted

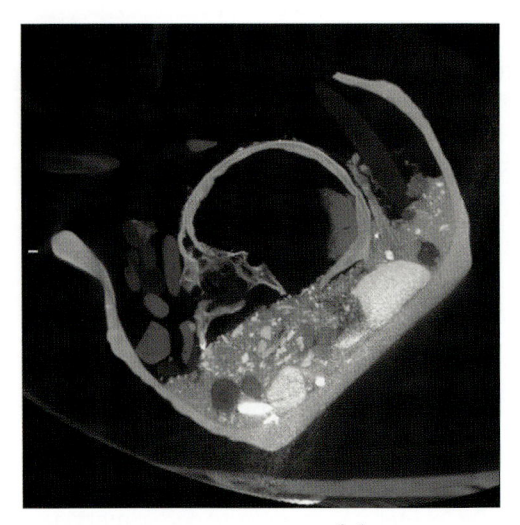

Fig. 6.8. A transverse section of the terra cotta pot demonstrating brain in the base of skull. The position of the brain indicates that Edwin D. Morgan was in a supine position when the brain dehydrated (Credit: Bioanthropology Research Institute, Quinnipiac University).

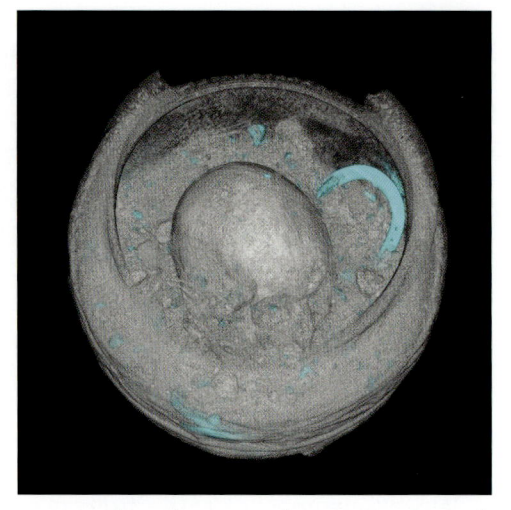

Fig. 6.9. Three-dimensional reconstruction with an algorithm applied to demonstrate metallic artifacts in blue. Note the position of one of the horseshoes (Bioanthropology Research Institute, Quinnipiac University).

Fig. 6.10. Wooden stake positioned in front of the skull with feathers adhering (Photo: Molly Rathbun).

on them (Fig. 6.10). A few of the twigs had small feathers attached as well as cut marks and dried blood from animal sacrifices (Rathbun 2013, 7).

When the sticks and feathers were removed, the superior portion of Edwin Denison Morgan's cranium was fully revealed. The skull was placed upright inside the pot with the basilar (underneath) section resting on a base of loamy soil overlying a distinct layer of fine beach sand on the bottom. A total of four rooster feet were found: One on top, one behind, and two underneath the skull. The skull and the beak of a chicken/rooster were recovered from the right parietal area, along with a clump of earth containing a clamshell (*Mercenaria mercenaria*). Two additional chicken beaks were positioned against the left occipital-parietal area, also interspersed within the soil (Fig. 6.11).

By Edwin's face was a wooden stake or cross with the point down and strands of bird feathers adhering to it. This object was found with additional sticks marked in red or blue ink. Writings in red were, "NAMO," "PIMO," "NADESTO," "MARIA," "IMITOMOKADO (IMITOMORADO?)," "BAMOBRA (RAMOBRA?), and "BENEATAKO". The one stick with

Fig. 6.11. Cluster of artifacts, including rooster skull and wax candle recovered from clay pot (Photo: Molly Rathbun).

blue text read, "CAMPECHE." All of these were written in upper case print. Another short stick was found underneath the skull once it had been removed and spelled, "ONUNO." "Campeche" is a State of Mexico on the Yucatan peninsula and "Maria", of course, is a woman's name and that of the Mother of Christ. None of the other words were decipherable to our team, though we assumed are interpretable in the Lucumi or Yoruba languages.

Numerous other objects were retrieved within the clay pot, including the those listed in order of recovery in Table 6.1.

It appears that the sand matrix, shellfish fragments and rounded water worn stones were taken together from a beach area along the Connecticut coast or at Black rock State Park as acknowledged by the suspect to be utilized within the cauldron. In addition

Table 6.1. Ritual objects retrieved within the clay pot listed in order of recovery.

Burial object	Quantity	Context
Ceramic shards	2	Superior to the skull
Sharpened sticks	20	Inserted around the rim
White feathers	7	Adhering to wooden stake/cross
Wooden stake/cross	1	Resting in front of face
Bird's feet #1	2	One posterior of occipital and one superior of the cranial vault; claws up
Short stakes	5	Posterior to the skull; inscribed
Rooster skull and beak #1	1	Right parietal area
Cigar butt #1	1	Right temporal area
Cigar #2	1	Left eye orbit
Cigar #3	1	Horizontally in front of face
Paper	1	Right eye orbit
Bird beak #2	1	Left posterior occipital/parietal
Coconut shell #1	1	Front of face under Cigar #3
Bird beak #3	1	
Bird feet #2	1	
Cellophane/plastic	1	
Bird feet #3	1	Underneath right side of skull
Bird feet #4	1	Underneath center of skull
Coconut shell #2	1	Underneath right side of skull
Soft-shelled Clam	1	Underneath left side of skull
Broken glass	1	Underneath center skull
Rooster skull #2	1	Underneath center skull and foramen magnum
Red candle with wax drippings	1	Underneath mandible
Scallop shell	1	Underneath skull
Round stone #1	1	Underneath skull; water worn
Wooden stake #6, rooster skull #4, candle wax, botanical nut	5	Clumped by wax under skull and mandible
Stone #2	1	Rounded water worn; under skull
Stone #3	1	Posterior to lower occipital
Horseshoe #1	1	Under posterior portion of skull with nails embedded
Horseshoe #2	1	Lower portion of face
Lincoln penny #1 (2002)	1	Posterior left side of skull embedded in sand
Lincoln penny #2 (1997)	1	Posterior left side
Lincoln penny #3 (1981)	1	Bottom center of vessel

Compiled by Molly Rathbun (2013)

to the artifacts recovered, white chalk crosses were etched around the interior of the vessel (Fig. 6.12).

All these ritual objects are consistent with the physiognomies of Palo Mayombe used to channel Aché energies during healing/harming ceremonies (Gill *et al.* 2009; Ochoa 2004; Kail 2008; Windburn *et al.* 2016). The use of a stolen human skull from a grave of a person powerful in life, the hiding away of the clay pot in a closet, the use of animal sacrifice, material culture and symbols to entice the spirit world, all suggest that the motive for the desecration of Edwin Denison Morgan Tomb and the subsequent pilfering of human remains was Palo Mayombe ritual.

Fig. 6.12. Interior of clay vessel showing white chalk crosses and two horseshoes. Note the blood drippings from the rim of the pot to the left and human mandible lower right (Photo: Molly Rathbun).

A ceremonial explanation for the tomb robbery seemed pretty clear but another mystery nagged at me. Why was Mary B.P. Morgan the only family member buried on the right side wall, and why was she was not interred next to her husband, Edwin Denison Morgan III? The rest of Governor Edwin Denison Morgan's immediate family was placed in vaults surrounding him on the center wall, including his wife and the four children that died young. However, Mary's husband was buried *outside* the tomb, not inside on the wall beside her. We found it peculiar that Mary reposed separately from the rest of the family and wondered more about who she was.

> Mary B.P. Morgan Vault # 1652 – Place of death, Newport, R.I.
> Last Residence New York City, Wife of E.D. Morgan,
> Buried in Lot 6 Section 12, Undertaker W.R. Morgan,
> Age 29, Date of Death August 18th 1886, Cause Typhoid Fever,
> Date of interment August 21st, 1886.
>
> Burial Card, Cedar Hill Cemetery, Hartford, Connecticut

He has been referred to as the "Gilded Age Poster Boy" (Fig. 6.13): Young, handsome, educated (Harvard Class of 1877), member of the Hasty Pudding Society, fraternal brother of Delta Kappa Epsilon, married (1880) and very, very rich (Half Pudding Society 2012). He was born Alfred Waterman Morgan named after his uncle who died during infancy. However, when his own father, Dr Edwin Denison Morgan II passed away in 1879, his grandfather, New York's Civil War governor, bade Alfred, his only surviving descendant, to legally change his name to Edwin Denison Morgan III, hence, maintaining the family lineage. Though he may not have wanted to amend his birth name, how could he refuse? Alfred/Edwin now stood poised to inherit a fortune valued at $12 million (about $400 million today) when his grandfather died. Since his grandparents had lost all their

Fig. 6.13. Edwin Denison Morgan III (1854-1933) (Credit: Appleton Morgan, A History of the Family Morgan, The City of New York: [1902]).

children as infants or in their young adult lives, the governor's will also provided for an additional $250,000 per legitimate offspring Edwin III could sire (Half Pudding Society 2012). Obviously, Governor Morgan was very concerned for the continuance of his name and family pedigree.

Alfred Waterman/Edwin Denison III was born in Throg's Neck, New York on 19 October 1854. After graduating from Harvard, he became a clerk in his grandfather's brokerage and worked himself up to a trustee of the business (Harvard College 1885). He married Mary, the daughter of George Henry Penniman and Margaret (nee Brewer) Penniman, in March 1880 at her father's Fifth Avenue mansion (*New York Tribune* 1880). The wedding, officiated by the Episcopal Rev. William F. Morgan, a relative of the groom, was remembered as a brilliant affair and the former governor was pleased with the new marriage alliance (*New York Herald* 1886). Edwin was 26 years old and Mary was 22. She was young, attractive and socially refined; he was wealthy and athletic. In 1885, they embarked on an around the world yachting excursion (*St Albans Daily Messenger* 1885), enjoying the life of privilege and escapade. Unfortunately, Edwin III's marriage to Mary B.P. Morgan turned out to be short-lived and without issue.

Mary was born on 1 June 1857 in New York City. Her father was a wealthy merchant who made his fortune from linseed oil and real estate. They lived at 536 Fifth Avenue, not far from the mansion of Governor Edwin Denison Morgan. We could find no record of how Edwin and Mary met, but they would have traveled in the same social circles since both families were considered aristocrats. The governor and his wife Eliza were apparently very fond of their new daughter-in-law and Mary was undoubtedly sophisticated, once referred to as "a most charming lady ... a great addition to all social gatherings" (*New York Times* 1886). She was also an excellent cross-country horsewoman, winning numerous honors on the hunting fields (*New York Herald* 1886).

In March of 1886, Mary and Edwin were returning from a trip to Europe onboard the *S.S. Oregon* when the ocean liner collided with a schooner off the coast of Long Island. Though the ship was approaching Fire Island and preparing to arrive in New York harbor, damage to the hull was extensive forcing the *Oregon* to list bow-first and start to sink.

Fortunately, all the passengers were rescued, including Edwin and Mary, but the trauma of the shipwreck haunted Mary for the few remaining months she had to live. It was reported that she lost over $30,000 in jewelry when the ship went down (*New York Herald* 1886).

Mary died later that summer (18 August 1886) at Newport, Rhode Island, in the villa mansion of a friend, Mrs Paran Stevens. She had developed a high fever a couple of weeks earlier that was diagnosed as typhoid, an affliction usually associated with the massed, urban poor rather than upper class Gilded Age socialites. No one thought her illness serious, not even her husband, and her health seemed to be improving right up to the time of her death. In fact, Edwin D. Morgan III had spent the day before she died playing polo and the day she died "steaming" his yacht, *Amy*, in Narragansett Bay (Vidette 1886). When he returned home about 6:30 pm, he was told that Mary had taken a turn for the worse. Earlier that day while plying the waters of the Bay, he confided to a colleague that he had had a premonition that bad news was in store for him and by the time he arrived at her bedside Mary was unconscious. Mary B.P. Morgan passed away around 9 pm that evening, she was only 29 years old and in the prime of a privileged life (*New York Times* 1886; *New York Herald* 1886).

All of Newport and New York City Society were in shock by the sudden death of such a beloved member of their community and many of the summer social festivities were cancelled in her honor (*New York Herald* 1886). Her parents were traveling in Europe when they received the heartbreaking news of their daughter's unexpected death. With her husband absent on his yacht, she was attended by two close friends, "Miss Binninger of New York City" and Jennie Yznaga, wife of Cuban-American banker, Fernando Yznaga. Both women comforted Mary in her last conscious moments (*New York Times* 1886). The Secretary of the Navy was among the dignitaries at her New York City funeral. Three days afterward, she was interred in the Morgan Tomb on the wall adjacent to her father-in-law, the former governor at Cedar Hill.

Edwin left for Europe 2 weeks after the funeral. He sold his horses and racing stable in Hempstead, Long Island, of which Mary was very fond (Half Pudding Society 2012), but maintained his yachting endeavors. A year and a half later, he would remarry to Elizabeth Mary Moran (11 April 1888) and together they would have six children extending the Morgan lineage that Mary B.P. was evidently unable to provide. Edwin, inheriting an additional $1,500,000 from his grandfather's will, devoted the rest of his life to business and became a celebrated yachtsman (Fig. 6.14). He would be named Commodore of the New York Yacht Club and served on that club's American Cup Committee (Morgan 1938). Four times his boats defended the world trophy (Bell 2017). Edwin died on 13 June 1933 in Vermont at the age of 79. He was buried outside the tomb built by his grandfather alongside his second wife and their immediate family, leaving Mary B.P. Morgan to reside alone on the right wall of the interior crypt.

Surprisingly, we could find no extant photographs or paintings of Mary B.P. Morgan. Other than general genealogical information and her newspaper obituaries, our research team could find scarce historical data on her. Mary Catherine Sonntag placed numerous requests to libraries and online genealogy sites seeking images of Mary Morgan, but with

Fig. 6.14. Edwin Dennison Morgan III's Centerboard Schooner Constellation, 1892 (Credit: Detroit Publishing Company photograph collection, Library of Congress).

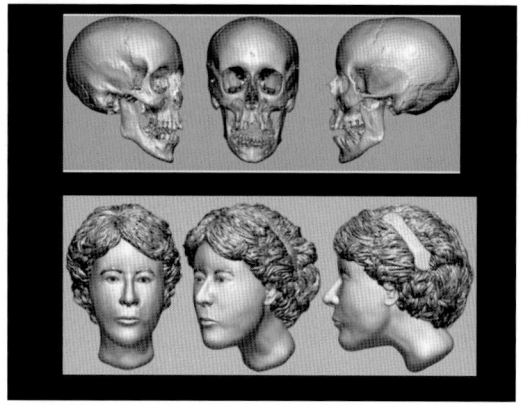

Fig. 6.15. Facial reconstruction of Mary B.P. Morgan from craniofacial remains. (Credit: Joe Mullins, George Mason University, Forensic Science).

no success. Meanwhile, the Quinnipiac University's Bioanthropology Research Institute (BRIQ) led by Jerry Conlogue and Tania Grgurich scanned Mary's cranium using 3D multi-detector computed tomography, creating a stereolithography (STL) file often utilized in producing an accurate model for facial approximation. Working with David Hunt at the Smithsonian Institution and Joe Mullins at George Mason University, a digital reconstruction of Mary B.P. Morgan's face was reproduced (Fig. 6.15).

****

Upon completion of the investigation, the grounds crew at Cedar Hill Cemetery reopened the Morgan Tomb for our final entry. We reinterred the skeleton remains of Governor Edwin Denison Morgan and his daughter-in-law Mary that had been removed during the tomb vandalism. They were replaced into their respective caskets in their original anatomical burial positions. When completed, the grounds crew positioned a concrete block at the tomb's entrance to secure it from further desecration.

Glossary

Compiled by James Hall

ad santo burial	Latin: "burial near the saints;" that is, adjacent to a church.
Adena Culture	The Adena culture was a Pre-Columbian Native American culture that existed from 800 BC to AD 1, in a time known as the Early Woodland period. The Adena culture refers to what were probably a number of related Native American societies sharing a burial complex and ceremonial system.
Adipocere	A grayish waxy substance formed by the decomposition of soft tissue in dead bodies subjected to moisture.
Affinal relationship	Those related to each other through marital relationship are called affinal kins or affines. The affinal kins are not related through the bond of blood. Also the kind of bond between spouses and their relatives on either side which arises out of legally defined marital relationship is known as affinal kinship.
Anaerobic bacteria	Bacteria that do not live or grow when oxygen is present. In humans, these bacteria are most commonly found in the gastro-intestinal tract.
Ankylosing spondylitis	An inflammatory disease that, over time, can cause some of the small bones in your spine (vertebrae) to fuse. This fusing makes the spine less flexible and can result in a hunched-forward posture.
Ante-mortem	Latin: "before death".
Anterior	Nearer the front, especially situated in the front of the body or nearer to the head.
Auditory canal	The ear canal, which is a pathway running from the outer ear to the middle ear.
Berm, earthen berm	A wall or parapet composed primarily of earth/soil.
Brass	An alloy of copper and zinc, in proportions which can be varied to achieve varying mechanical and electrical properties. It is a substitutional alloy: atoms of the two constituents may replace each other within the same crystal structure.
Calcaneus bone	The heel bone.
Callus (in bone)	Callus, also spelled callous, in osteology, bony and cartilaginous material forming a connecting bridge across a bone fracture during repair. Within 1–2 weeks after injury, a provisional callus forms, enveloping the fracture site.
Cary, caries	Decay and crumbling of a tooth or bone. Also referred to as cavities or tooth decay.
Cenotaph	A monument to someone buried elsewhere, especially one commemorating people who died in a war.

Cervical vertebrae	The cervical vertebrae of the spine consist of seven bony rings that reside in the neck between the base of the skull and the thoracic vertebrae in the trunk. Among the vertebrae of the spinal column, the cervical vertebrae are the thinnest and most delicate bones.
Church: Anglican	The Church of England, or Anglican Church, is the primary state church in England, where the concepts of church and state are linked. While the Church upholds many of the customs of Roman Catholicism, it also embraces fundamental ideas adopted during the Protestant Reformation.
Church: Congregational	Congregational churches (also Congregationalist churches; Congregationalism) are Protestant churches in the Reformed tradition practicing Congregationalist church governance, in which each congregation independently and autonomously runs its own affairs.
Church: and – Great Puritan Migration	The Great Puritan Migration was a period in the 17th century during which English puritans migrated to New England, the Chesapeake and the West Indies. English migration to Massachusetts consisted of a few hundred pilgrims who went to Plymouth Colony in the 1620s and between 13,000 and 21,000 emigrants who went to the Massachusetts Bay Colony between 1630 and 1642. The Puritans left England primarily due to religious persecution but also for economic reasons. England was in religious turmoil in the early 17th century, the religious climate was hostile and threatening, especially towards religious nonconformists like the puritans. The Puritans were a sect of religious dissidents who felt the Church of England (Anglican Church) was too closely associated with the Catholic religion and needed to be reformed.
Clavicle bone	The collar bone.
Computed Tomography (CT)	Refers to a computerized x-ray imaging procedure in which a narrow beam of X-rays is aimed at a patient and quickly rotated around the body, producing signals that are processed by the machine's computer to generate cross-sectional images ("slices") of the body.
Consanguineal relationship	Those who are related to each other by "blood' are known as consanguineal kin or cognates and the relationship based on blood-ties is called consanguineous (same blood) kinship.
Cortical bone/ surface	Cortical bone is the dense outer surface of bone that forms a protective layer around the internal cavity. This type of bone also known as compact bone makes up nearly 80% of skeletal mass and is imperative to body structure and weight bearing because of its high resistance to bending and torsion.
Cranial suture closures	The posterior fontanelle usually closes by age 1 or 2 months. It may already be closed at birth. The anterior fontanelle usually closes sometime between 9 and 18 months. The sutures and fontanelles are needed for the infant's brain growth and development.
Cranial vault	Also known as the skull vault, skullcap or calvaria, is the cranial space that encases and protects the brain.
Cranium	The part of the skull surrounding the brain. There are eight cranial bones – frontal bones, occipital bone, ethmoid bone, two parietal bones and temporal bones, and sphenoid bone. Together, they form a bony wall around the brain.

Glossary

Dessication	The act or process of drying something or the state of being or becoming dried up; the removal or loss of moisture; thorough drying.
Diffuse Idiopathic Skeletal Hyperostosis (DISH)	A type of arthritis that affects tendons and ligaments, mainly around your spine. These bands of tissue can become hardened (calcified) and form growths called bone spurs where they connect to your bones.
Disarticulated bones	Bones separated at the joints.
Distal end of femur bone	The distal femur is where the bone flares out like an upside-down funnel. The distal femur is the area of the leg just above the knee joint. Distal femur fractures most often occur either in older people whose bones are weak, or in younger people who have high energy injuries, e.g. from a car crash.
Ectocranial suture closure	A method of estimating age at death by comparing the degree of closure for cranial sutures on the outside of the skull (ectocranial, as opposed to endocranial, on the inside). These are compared to a baseline of over 300 measurements; and have been shown to be independent of race and sex.
Edentulous	Lacking teeth.
Enamel hypoplasia	A defect of the enamel that only occurs while teeth are still developing. Still, it can affect both baby teeth and permanent teeth. The condition results in thin enamel, which makes your teeth vulnerable to dental decay.
Epitaph	A phrase or form of words written in memory of a person who has died, especially as an inscription on a tombstone.
Exfoliation	The process of removing dead skin cells from the surface of your skin using a chemical, granular substance, or exfoliation tool.
Femur bone	The bone of the thigh or upper hind limb, articulating at the hip and the knee.
Fibula bone	The long, thin and lateral bone of the lower leg. It runs parallel to the Tibia, or shin bone, and plays a significant role in stabilizing the ankle and supporting the muscles of the lower leg.
Finial	A distinctive ornament at the apex of a roof, pinnacle, canopy or similar structure; an ornament at the top, end or corner of an object such as a post, piece of furniture, etc.
First Great Awakening	The First Great Awakening (sometimes Great Awakening) or the Evangelical Revival was a series of Christian revivals that swept Britain and its 13 North American colonies in the 1730s and 1740s.
Fisk Metallic Burial Case	Patented in 1848 by Almond Dunbar Fisk and originally manufactured in Providence, Rhode Island, the Fisk casket – unlike hexagonal wooden coffins or rectangular metal caskets – was shaped to conform firmly to human anatomy lying in a supine position: rounded head, extending out to wide shoulders, tapering in to a narrow waist, flaring pelvis and slimming to upward pointing feet. A "viewing glass" allowed the face to be seen during the funeral without the need to open the coffin lid, hence minimizing the removal of funerary souvenirs (i.e., hair lockets, etc.) from the dead and guaranteeing the least corruption of the deceased's body in its wait for the Day of Resurrection. A nameplate was situated over the crossed arms at the chest giving identity to the person within.
Foramen magnum	A large hole at the base of the skull in which the spinal cord enters the brain.

Foramina (cranial)	An opening that allows the passage of structures from one region to another. In the skull there are numerous foramina that transmit cranial nerves, blood vessels and other structures which are collectively referred to as the cranial foramina.
Forensic analysis	Refers to a detailed investigation for detecting and documenting the course, reasons, culprits, and consequences of a security incident or violation of rules of the organization or state laws. Forensic analysis is often linked with evidence to the court, particularly in criminal matters
French and Indian War	Also known as the Seven Years' War, this New World conflict marked another chapter in the long imperial struggle between Britain and France. When France's expansion into the Ohio River valley brought repeated conflict with the claims of the British colonies, a series of battles led to the official British declaration of war in 1756. Boosted by the financing of future Prime Minister William Pitt, the British turned the tide with victories at Louisbourg, Fort Frontenac and the French-Canadian stronghold of Quebec. At the 1763 peace conference, the British received the territories of Canada from France and Florida from Spain, opening the Mississippi Valley to westward expansion.
Friable (bone)	Easily crumbled.
Gracile	Gracefully slender or thin, esp. in an attractive manner.
Greater trochanter	A powerful protrusion located at the proximal (near) and lateral (outside) part of the shaft of the femur.
Harris lines	Growth arrest lines, also known as Harris lines, are lines of increased bone density that represent the position of the growth plate at the time of insult to the organism and formed on long bones due to growth arrest. They are only visible by radiograph or in cross-section.
Hopewell Culture	The Hopewell tradition (also called the Hopewell culture) describes the common aspects of the Native American culture that flourished along rivers in the north-eastern and mid-western Eastern Woodlands from 100 BCE to 500 CE, in the Middle Woodland period.
Humerus bone	A long bone in the arm that runs from the shoulder to the elbow. It connects the scapula and the two bones of the lower arm, the radius and ulna, and consists of three sections.
in situ	Latin: "in the original place".
King Philip's War	King Philip's War (also called the First Indian War, Metacom's War, Metacomet's War, Pometacomet's Rebellion, or Metacom's Rebellion) was an armed conflict in 1675–1678 between indigenous inhabitants of New England and New England colonists and their indigenous allies. The war is named for Metacomet, the Wampanoag chief who adopted the name Philip because of the friendly relations between his father Massasoit and the *Mayflower* Pilgrims. The war continued in the most northern reaches of New England until the signing of the Treaty of Casco Bay in April 1678.
Lintel	A horizontal support of timber, stone, concrete, or steel across the top of a door or window.
Malleolus bones	The lower portions of the Fibula bone (the Lateral Malleolus) and Tibia bone (the Medial Malleolus) which are connected to the Talus of the foot.
Mandible bone	The lower jawbone in mammals.

Mandibular condyles	The mandibular condyle forms articulation with the mandibular fossa of the temporal bone, called temporo-mandibular joint (TMJ).
Mastoid process bone	A pyramidal bony projection from the posterior section of the temporal bone.
Maxillary suture	The point of interface between the palates which form the roof of the mouth.
Medial	In anatomy, situated near the median plane of the body or the midline of an organ.
Musketaquid	The name Musketaquid honors the wisdom of Concord's first people who described this place according to its nature, "the place where the waters flow through the grasses."
Nasion	Also known as bridge of the nose, this is the midline bony depression between the eyes where the frontal and two nasal bones meet.
Occipital bone	The trapezoid-shaped bone at the lower-back of the cranium (skull). The occipital bone houses the back part of the brain and is one of seven bones that come together to form the skull.
Occipital condyle	The occipital condyles are two large protuberances on the undersurface of the occipital bone, located besides the front half of the foramen magnum. It forms the connection between the skull and the vertebral column.
Occlusal tooth surfaces	The chewing surface of posterior teeth.
Ossification	The process of laying down new bone material by cells called osteoblasts. It is synonymous with bone tissue formation.
Osteomyelitis	An infection of the bone, a rare but serious condition. Bones can become infected in a number of ways: Infection in one part of the body may spread through the bloodstream into the bone, or an open fracture or surgery may expose the bone to infection.
Osteoporosis	A medical condition in which the bones become brittle and fragile from loss of tissue, typically as a result of hormonal changes, or deficiency of calcium or vitamin D.
Osteoarthritis	Degeneration of joint cartilage and the underlying bone, most common from middle age onward. It causes pain and stiffness, especially in the hip, knee, and thumb joints.
Palate	The roof of the mouth, separating the cavities of the nose and the mouth in vertebrates.
Patella bone	Also known as the kneecap, is a flat, circular-triangular bone which articulates with the femur (thigh bone) and covers and protects the anterior articular surface of the knee joint.
Pathology	The study of the causes and effects of disease or injury. The word pathology also refers to the study of disease in general, incorporating a wide range of bioscience research fields and medical practices.
Pelvis	The large bony structure near the base of the spine to which the hind limbs or legs are attached in humans and many other vertebrates.
Periodontal	Relating to or affecting the structures surrounding and supporting the teeth.

Periosteum/ periosteal surface	A membrane that covers the outer surface of all bones, except at the articular surfaces (i.e. the parts within a joint space) of long bones.
Pewter	A malleable metal alloy composed of 85–99% tin, mixed with approximately 5–10% antimony, 2% copper, bismuth, and sometimes silver. Copper and antimony act as hardeners but may be replaced with lead in lower grades of pewter, imparting a bluish tint.
Physiognomy	A person's facial features or expression, especially when regarded as indicative of character or ethnic origin.
Plane radiography	A means of obtaining a picture of internal structures by passing X-rays through them, and recording the shadows cast by these structures.
Posterior	Further back in position; of or nearer the rear or hind end, especially of the body or a part of it.
Post-mortem	Latin: "after death".
Proximal end of femur	The proximal aspect of the femur articulates with the acetabulum of the pelvis to form the hip joint. It consists of a head and neck, and two bony processes – the greater and lesser trochanters.
Radial tuberosity	An oval eminence on the medial side of the radius bone where the tendon of the biceps muscle inserts.
Radius bone	This is one of the two large bones of the forearm, the other being the ulna. It extends from the lateral side of the elbow to the thumb side of the wrist and runs parallel to the ulna. The ulna is usually slightly longer than the radius, but the radius is thicker.
Sacroiliac joint	Connects the hip bones (iliac crests) to the sacrum, the triangular bone between the lumbar spine and the tailbone (coccyx). The primary function of the sacroiliac joints is to absorb shock between the upper body and the pelvis and legs.
Sacrum bone	The sacrum is a large wedge shaped vertebra at the inferior end of the spine. It forms the solid base of the spinal column where it intersects with the hip bones to form the pelvis. The sacrum is a very strong bone that supports the weight of the upper body as it is spread across the pelvis and into the legs.
Santeria	Santería, also known as *Regla de Ocha*, *Regla Lucumí*, or *Lucumí*, is an Afro-American religion that developed in Cuba between the 16th and 19th centuries. It arose through a process of syncretism between the traditional Yoruba religion of West Africa and the Roman Catholic form of Christianity.
Saponification	A process that involves conversion of fat, oil or lipid into soap and alcohol by the action of heat in the presence of aqueous alkali.
Scapula bone	Also known as the shoulder bone or shoulder blade, this is the bone that connects the humerus (upper arm bone) with the clavicle (collar bone).
Schematic diagram	A picture that represents the components of a process, device, or other object using abstract, often standardized symbols and lines.
Shellac	A resin secreted by the female lac bug on trees in the forests of India and Thailand. It is processed and sold as dry flakes and dissolved in alcohol to make liquid shellac, which is used as a brush-on colorant, food glaze and wood finish.

Glossary

Staffordshire pottery	Most Staffordshire pottery pieces are easy to recognize. They have a brightly colored painted form and even clear glaze over a strong and sturdy ceramic body. They often have blue/white transferware decorations on them featuring famous places, military battle sites, and important figures. Production began in the early 18th century.
Stereolithography (STL)	A form of 3D printing technology used for creating models, prototypes, patterns, and production parts in a layer by layer fashion using photochemical processes to form polymers, which then make up the body of a three-dimensional solid.
Stratigraphic position	Stratigraphy is a branch of geology concerned with the study of rock layers (strata) and layering (stratification). It is primarily used in the study of sedimentary and layered volcanic rocks. Generally: the lower the layer, the older it is.
Stucco	A fine plaster used for coating wall surfaces or molding into architectural decorations.
Supraorbital ridge	The brow ridge, which refers to a bony ridge located above the eye sockets (orbits) of all primates. In modern humans the eyebrows are located on their lower margin.
Tibia bone	The larger, stronger, and anterior (frontal) of the two bones in the leg below the knee in vertebrates (the other being the fibula, behind and to the outside of the tibia), and it connects the knee with the ankle bones.
Tuberculosis	Tuberculosis (TB) is caused by a bacterium called *Mycobacterium tuberculosis*. The bacteria usually attack the lungs, but TB bacteria can attack any part of the body such as the kidney, spine, and brain. Not everyone infected with TB bacteria becomes sick. As a result, two TB-related conditions exist: latent TB infection (LTBI) and TB disease. If not treated properly, TB disease can be fatal.
Ulna bone	The ulna is a long bone found in the forearm that stretches from the elbow to the smallest finger, and when in anatomical position, is found on the medial side of the forearm. It runs parallel to the radius, the other long bone in the forearm.
Ziegler Coffin/ Transfer Case	The Ziegler case, also called a body or disaster transfer case is used for transporting human remains without a casket. These cases are constructed out of 20 gauge steel with a channel gasket in the lid and. are hermetically sealed with screws.

Bibliography

Allison, N. (2018) After Andrew Jackson's grave was vandalized, crews are trying to restore it, *The Tennessean*. https://eu.tennessean.com/story/news/2018/05/10/crews-work-restore-andrew-jacksons-grave-after-graffiti-vandalism/600320002/.

Anon. (1883) *In Memoriam, Edwin Denison Morgan. Born Feb. 3d, 1811. Died Feb. 14th, 1883*. New York: J.H. Huth.

Anon. (1903) *Cedar Hill Cemetery, Hartford Connecticut 1863-1903*. Hartford CT: Cedar Hill Cemetery.

Armstrong, T. (2018) *Thomas Hardy: Selected Poems*. Philadelphia PA, Routledge.

Barbian, L. and Sledzik, P. (2005) *Pathological Analysis of Skeletal Elements from the Bulkeley Family Tomb, Colchester*, Connecticut. Storrs CT: unpublished report, Office of State Archaeology, University of Connecticut.

Bastis, K. (2006) *Health, Wealth and Available Material: The Bioarchaeology of the Bulkeley Tomb in Colchester, Connecticut*. Unpublished MA Thesis, University of Connecticut.

Bass, W. (1987) *Human Osteology: A Laboratory and Field Manual* (3rd edn). Columbia MO: Missouri Archaeological Society.

Beers, J. B. (1884) *History of Middlesex County, Connecticut with Biographical Sketches of its Prominent Men*. New York: J.B. Beers.

Bell, B. A. (2017) Edwin Dennison Morgan III's Farmed Racing Yacht "Constellation" Was Built in a Pelham Shipyard in 1889, http://www.historicpelham.blogspot.com, Archive of the Historic Pelham Web Site, 14 December.

Bellantoni, N. F. (1991a) *Letter to Sergeant Mitchell Ward, Middletown Police Department, Human Cranium Case No. 91-0755*, 12 August. Author.

Bellantoni, N. F. (1991b) *Letter to Sergeant Mitchell Ward, Middletown Police Department, Chauncey Family Crypt Vandalism, Case No. 91-17738*, 11 September. Author.

Bellantoni, N. F. (1993) *Field Notes for the Chauncey Tomb Investigation*. Storrs CT: unpublished manuscript on file Office of State Archaeology, University of Connecticut.

Bellantoni, N. (2000) *Field Notes from the Pitkin Family Tomb*. Storrs CT: unpublished manuscript on file with the Office of State Archaeology, University of Connecticut.

Bellantoni, N. F. (2003) *Huntington Re-Entombment Project, Field Notes*. Storrs CT: unpublished report Office of State Archaeology, University of Connecticut.

Bellantoni, N. F. and Cooke, D. G. (1997) Forensic archaeology at the Chauncey family crypt, Indian Hill Cemetery, Middletown, Connecticut. In Poirier and Bellantoni (eds), 173–184.

Bellantoni, N. F. and Spaulding, J. J. (2002) *The Tomb of Gershom Bulkeley and His Descendants: A pictorial review of the investigation of the Gershom Bulkeley Tomb in the Old Cemetery on Stebbins Rd., Colchester, Connecticut*. Colchester CT: unpublished pictorial binder Cragin Library.

Bettelheim, J. (2001) Palo Monte Mayombe and its influence on Cuban contemporary art. *African Arts* 34 (2) 36–49, 94–96.

Bickle, P., Cummings, V., Hofmann, D. and Pollard, J. (2017) *The Neolithic of Europe*. Oxford: Oxbow Books.

Blau, S. and Ubelaker, D. H. (eds) (2016) *Handbook of Forensic Anthropology and Archaeology*. New York: Routledge.

Brandon, G. (2012) Lucumi divination, the mythic world and the management of misfortune. *Anthropologica* 54 (2).

Brown, A. (2018) A new generation of L.A. Satanists finds community in blasphemous times. *Los Angeles Times*, 5 January.

Brown, B. (1976) *Flintlocks and Barrels of Beef: Colchester, Connecticut and the American Revolution*. Colchester, CT: Bacon Academy.

Bulkeley, Rev. J. (1725) An inquiry into the rights of the Aboriginal Natives to the lands of America, and titles derived from them. In: Wolcott, R. *Poetical Mediations, being the improvement of some vacant hours, by Roger Wolcott, Esq; with a preface by the Reverend Mr. Bulkley of Colchester*, New London CT, L. Green.

Bushnell, E. (1796) *Letter to Roger Griswold*. New Haven CT: Yale University, William Griswold Lane Collection, Box 13, Sterling Memorial Library, 24 January.

Cabrera, L. (1983) *El Monte*. Miami FL: Universal Press (first published 1854).

Challos, C. (1997) Lincoln's tomb gets 24-hour guard after spray-painted vandalism, *Chicago Tribune*, 27 February. https://www.chicagotribune.com/news/ct-xpm-1997-02-25-9702250145-story.html.

Chandler, R. J. and Potash, S. J. (2007) *Gold, Silk, Pioneers and Mail: The Story of the Pacific Mail Steamship Company*. San Francisco CA: Friends of the San Francisco Maritime Museum Library.

Chapman, F. W. (1875) *The Bulkeley Family; or the Descendants of Rev. Peter Bulkeley, Who Settled at Concord, Mass., in 1636*. Compiled at the request of Joseph E. Bulkeley, Hartford CT: Case, Lockeood & Brainard.

Chicago Tribune (2000) Civil War grave robbed in suspected satanic ritual, www.chicagotribune.com, 23 June.

Chorlton, T. P. (2011) *The First American Republic 1774–1789: The First Fourteen American Presidents Before Washington*. Authorhouse Publishing.

Church, D. (2005) Secrets of forgotten Bulkeley Tomb revealed. *Regional Standard*, 15 April.

Constitution, The (1863) Local News, Died, Middletown, Connecticut, 6 May.

Cronon, W. (1983) *Changes in the Land: Indians, Colonists, and the Ecology of New England*, New York: Hill and Wang.

Cruson, D. (2011) *Putnam's Revolutionary War Winter Encampment: The History and Archaeology of Putnam Memorial State Park*. Charleston SC: The History Press.

Cunliffe, B. (2001) *The Oxford Illustrated History of Prehistoric Europe* (revised edn). Oxford: Oxford University Press.

Daly, M. E. (2002) Disease and our ancestors: Mortality in the eighteenth and nineteenth centuries. *New England Ancestry* 3, 5–6.

Daniels, B. C. (1975) *Connecticut's First Family: William Pitkin and His Connections*. Chester CT, Pequot Press.

New York Evangelist (1886) Deaths. Morgan at Newport, 2 Sept., 5.

Deseret News (2000) Authorities think skull theft may be part of satanic rite, www.deseret.com, 23 June.

Devino, K. (2003) *The Bulkeley Family: A Look at the Family, Colchester and Connecticut in the Seventeenth, Eighteenth and Nineteenth Centuries*. Colchester CT: unpublished report, Colchester Historical Society.

Dexter, F. B. (1911) *Biographical Sketches of the Graduates of Yale College With Annals of the College History, vol. v. July 1178–June 1792*. New York: Henry Holt and Company.

Dimmick, L. (1999) *American Sculpture in the Metropolitan Museum of Art: A Catalogue of Works by Artists Born Before 1865*. New York: Metropolitan Museum of Art.

Doolittle, J. and Bellantoni, N. F. (2010) The search for graves with ground-penetrating radar in Connecticut. *Journal of Archaeological Science* 37, 941–949.

Dryfhout, J. H. (2008) *The Works of Augustus Saint-Gaudens*. Lebanon NH: University of New England Press.

East Oregonian (2014) Out of the vault: Grave-robbing leads to fears of satanic cult, www.eastoregonian.com, 20 September.

Elliot, N. (2014) *Henry Chauncey: An American Life*, New York: Peter Lang.
Ellis, W. (2018) Legend trips and Satanism: Adolescents' ostensive traditions as "cult" activity. In: McNeil, L. and Tucker, E. (eds), *Legend Tripping: A Contemporary Legend Casebook* Louisville CO: University Press of Colorado, 94–111.
Federal Writers' Project (1938) *Connecticut: A Guide to Its Roads, Lore and People*, Works Progress Administration for the State of Connecticut. American Guide Series. Boston, Houghton Mifflin/U.S. History Publishers.
Foster, L. (2003) Re-burial of the 'first president', *Hartford Courant*, 25 November. https://www.courant.com/news/connecticut/hc-xpm-2003-11-25-0311250867.
Fowler, W. C. (1858) *Memorials of the Chaunceys, Including President Chauncey, His Ancestors and Descendants*. Boston: Henry W. Dutton & Sons.
Fowler, W. C. (1866) *History of Durham, Connecticut, From the First Grant of Land in 1662 to 1866*. Hartford CT: Waterman & Eaton Press.
French, S. (1974) The cemetery as cultural institution: The establishment of Mount Auburn & the "rural cemetery" movement, *American Quarterly* 26 (1), 37–59.
Gerlach, L. R. (1976) *Connecticut congressman: Samuel Huntington, 1731-1796*. Connecticut Bicentennial Series XX, Hartford CT: The American Revolution Bicentennial Commission of Connecticut.
Gill, J. R., Rainwater, C. W. and Bradley, M. S. (2009) Santeria and Palo Mayombe: Skulls, mercury and artifacts. *Journal of Forensic Sciences* 54 (6), 1458–1462.
Goodwin, J. O. (1879) *East Hartford: Its History and Traditions*. Hartford CT: Case, Lockwood & Brainard.
Half Pudding Society (2012) *Gilded Age Poster Boy*. http://www.halfpuddinghalksauce.blogspot.com, 22 April.
Hardy, T. (1920) *The Collective Poems of Thomas Hardy*. New York, Macmillan, 361–364.
Harper, R. (2005) *Coffin Hardware from the Bulkeley Tomb, Colchester, Connecticut*. Storrs CT: Unpublished Report, Office of State Archaeology, University of Connecticut.
Harvard College, Class of 1877 (1885) *Secretary's Report, No. III*, Abington MA: Press of the Abington Herald, 77.
Hill, N. (2006) The transformation of the Lincoln Tomb. *Journal of the Abraham Lincoln Association* 27 (1), 39–56.
Huntington Family Association (1915) *The Huntington Family in America; A Genealological Memoir of the Known Descendants of Simon Huntington from 1633 to 1915, Including Those Who Have Retained the Family Name and Many Bearing Other Surnames*. Hartford CT: Huntington Family Association.
Jackes, M.K. (1983) Osteological evidence for smallpox: a possible case from seventeenth century Ontario. *American Journal of Physical Anthropology* 60, 75–81.
Jackson, C. O. (1977) American attitudes to death. *Journal of American Studies* 11 (3), 297–312.
Jacobus, D. L. (1933) *The Bulkeley Genealogy, The Descendants of the Rev. Peter Bulkeley*. New Haven CT: Tuttle, Morehouse & Taylor.
Jodziewicz, T. W. (1988) A stranger in the land: Gershom Bulkeley of Connecticut. *Transactions of the American Philosophical Society* 78 (2).
Kail, T. M. (2008) *Magico-Religious Groups and Ritualistic Activities: A Guide for First Responders*. Boca Raton FL: CRC Press.
Kemble, J. H. (1943) *The Panama Route 1848-1869*. Los Angeles CA: University of California Press.
Klepinger, L. L. (2010) Unusual skeletal anomalies and pathologies in forensic casework. In: Fairgrieve, S. I. (ed.), *Forensic Osteological Analysis: A Book of Case Studies*. Springfield IL: Charles C. Thomas, 226–236.
Kosmin, B., Mayer, E. and Keysar, A. (2001) *American Religious Identification Survey*, New York: Graduate Center of the City University of New York.
Kostof, S. (1995) *A History of Architecture*. Oxford: Oxford University Press.

Kranhold, K. (1992) Archaeologist digs into the desecration of a family plot. *The Hartford Courant*, Section C, 16 April, 1.

Krogman, W. M. and Yasar Iscan, M. (1986) *The Human Skeleton in Forensic Medicine* 2nd edn. Springfield IL: Charles C. Thomas.

Lavin, L. (ed.) (2017) Special Thematic Issue: The Wangunk Tribal Communities of the Lower Connecticut River Valley. *Bulletin of the Archaeological Society of Connecticut* 79.

Lester, K. (2015) Illinois' financial crisis is ruining Abe Lincoln's tomb, Associated Press, *Business Insider*, 15 April. https://www.businessinsider.com/illinois-financial-crisis-is-ruining-abe-lincolns-tomb-2015-4?r=US&IR=T.

Llewellyn, J. F. (1998) *A Cemetery Should BE Forever: The Challenge to Managers and Directors*. Glendale CA: Tropico Press.

Ludwig, A. (1999) *Graven Images: New England Stonecarving and Its Symbols, 1650-1815*. Middletown CT: Wesleyan University Press.

Lynott, M. (2015) *Hopewell Ceremonial Landscapes of Ohio*. American Landscapes Series. Oxford: Oxbow Books.

McCabe, F. (2004) Historian makes presidential case. *Norwich Bulletin* 19, Feburary, 1.

McCullough, D. (1977) *The Path Between the Seas: The Creation of the Panama Canal 1870-1914*. New York: Simon and Schuster.

McRae, O. (2004) A history of the American cemetery. *American Cemetery*, August, 30–36.

McShane, L. (2019) Graffiti, peeling paint, stained ceilings: Ulysses S. Grant's final resting place needs a makeover and fast, with the 200th anniversary of his birth approaching, *New York Dailey News*, 28 April. https://www.nydailynews.com/new-york/ny-grants-tomb-problems-20190428.

McWeeney, L. (2005) *Coffin Materials Analysis for the Bulkeley Tomb*. Storrs CT: unpublished manuscript Office of State Archaeology, University of Connecticut.

Miller, T. (2013) *The Lost Edwin D. Morgan Mansion - No. 411 Fifth Avenue*. http://www.datoninmanhattan.blogspot.com.

Moomaw, G. (2015) Monroe's tomb to be repaired in advance of 200th anniversary of his election as president, *Richmond Times-Dispatch*, 29 September.

Morgan, A. (1902) *The History of the Family of Morgan From the Year 1089 to the Present Times*. New York: City of New York.

Morgan, E. D. III (1938) *Recollections of My Family*, New York: Scribner & Sons.

Morse, D., Duncan, J. and Stoutamire, J. (1983) *Handbook of Forensic Archaeology and Anthropology*. Tallahassee FL: Florida State University Foundation.

Murphy, K. (2010) *Crowbar Governor: The Life and Times of Morgan Gardner Bulkeley*. Middletown CT: Wesleyan University Press.

Myjer, I. (2003) *Conditions Assessment and Treatment Recommendation for the Governor Samuel Huntington Tomb, Norwich Colonial Burial Ground, Norwich, Connecticut*. Storrs CT: unpublished report Office of State Archaeology, University of Connecticut.

New York Herald (1886) Mrs. E.D. Morgan Dead: Newport Society Saddened by the Unexpected Intelligence, 19 August, 1.

New York Times (1883) Edwin D. Morgan, 15 February, 1.

New York Times (1886) Mrs. Edwin D. Morgan Dead: Shock for Society in Newport and New-York, 19 August, 1.

New York Tribune (1880) Married, 16 March.

Ochoa, T. R. (2004) Aspects of the dead. In: Font, M. A. (ed.), *Cuba Today: Continuity and Change Since the "Periodo Especial"*. New York: Bidner Center for Western Hemispheric Studies, Graduate Center of the City University of New York, 245–260.

Olivieri, I., D'Angelo, S., Palazzi, C., Padula, A., Mader, R. and Khan, M. A. (2009) Diffuse idiopathic skeletal hyperostosis: Differentiation from ankylosing spondylitis. *Current Rheumatology Reports* 11 (5), 321–328.

Olson-Raymer, G. (1989) *Research Update, Special Edition, Occult Crime: A Law Enforcement Primer.* Sacramento CA: Office of Criminal Justice Planning, State of California 1 (6).

Paleopathology Association (1991) *Skeletal Database Committee Recommendations.* Detroit: Paleopathology Association.

Petry, L. (1992) Police charge man with vandalizing city crypt. *The Middletown Press*, 22 April, 1.

Pfeiffer, S., Milne, S. and Stevenson, R. (1998) The natural decomposition of adipocere. *Journal of Forensic Sciences* 43, 368–370.

Pitkin, A.P. (1887) *Pitkin Family of America*. Hartford CT: Case, Lockwood & Brainard.

Poirier, D. A. and Bellantoni, N. F. (1997) *In Remembrance: Archaeology and Death*. Westport CT: Bergin & Garvey.

Pokines, J. T. and Baker, J. E. (2013) Effects of burial environment on osseous remains. In: Pokines, J. and Symes, S. A. (eds), *Manual of Forensic Taphonom*. Boca Raton FL, CRC Press, 73–114.

Poteet, J. M. (1975) Unrest in the "Land of Steady Habits": The Hartford Riot of 1722. *Proceedings of the American Philosophical Society* 119 (3), 223–232.

Ransom, D. F. (1996) Cedar Hill Cemetery, Hartford, Connecticut. *National Register of Historic Places Form*. Hartford CT: on file with State Historical Preservation Office, 6.

Rathbun, M. (2013) *Excavation of Santeria Ritual Pot and Investigation of Morgan Tomb Robbery*. Storrs CT: unpublished manuscript on file, Office of State Archaeology, University of Connecticut.

Rawley, J. A. (1968) *Edwin D. Morgan, 1811-1883: Merchant in Politics*. New York: AMS Press.

Reeson, A. (2015) *Tombstone Technology*, http://www.summit-memorials.blogspot.com, posted 19 January.

Robertson, P. (1982) The plot to steal Lincoln's body. *American Heritage* 33, 3.

Scaturro, F. (2017) Restore Grant's Tomb to its glory – and other National Park treasures, too. *New York Daily News*, 26 April.

Slater, J. (1987) *The Colonial Burying Grounds of Eastern Connecticut and the Men Who Made Them*. Hamden CT: Memoirs of the Connecticut Academy of Arts & Sciences 21, Archon Books.

Sledzik, P. S. and Hunt, D. R. (1997) Disaster and relief efforts at the Hardin Cemetery. In: Poirier and Bellantoni (eds) 1997, 185–196.

Sobel, R. and Raimo, J. (eds) (1978) *Biographical Directory of the Governors of the United States, 1789-1978*, vol. 3. Westport CT: Meckler Books.

Solecki, R. S. (1975) Shanidar IV, a Neanderthal flower burial in northern Iraq. *Science* 190 (4217), 880–801.

Spaulding, J. J. (2001) *Squire Elisha Pitkin Vault, East Hartford*. Storrs CT: unpublished manuscript, Office of State Archaeology, University of Connecticut.

Spaulding, J. J. (2006) *Gershom Bulkeley & His Descendants*. Storrs CT: unpublished report, Office of State Archaeology, University of Connecticut.

Spaulding, J. J. and Bellantoni, N. F. (2001) Who is buried in the "empty" vault? *Quarterly Newsletter of the Association of Gravestone Studies* 25 (2), 3–6.

St Albans Daily Messenger (1885) Rich Women of New York, 21 March.

Stannard, D. E. (1977) *The Puritan Way of Death*. New York: Oxford University Press.

Stannard, D. E. (1980) Where all our steps are tending: Death in the American context. In: Pike, M. and Armstrong, J. G. *A Time To Mourn: Expressions of Grief in Nineteenth Century America*. New York: Museums at Stony Brook.

State of Connecticut General Statutes, "Human Burials," Section 10-388, https://www.cga.ct.gov/current/pub/chap_184a.htm#sec_10-388.

Stephens, J. L. (1849) *Letter to Henry Chauncey*. Washington DC: Georgetown University Library, Booth Family Center for Special Collections, 21 April.

Strong, J. (1796) *A Sermon Delivered at the Funeral of His Excellency Samuel Huntington, Governor of the State of Connecticut*. Hartford CT: Hudson & Goodwin.

Tilton, G. L. (1908) The grading of cemeteries. *Proceedings of the Convention of the American Association of Cemetery Superintendents* XXII.

UNESCO World Heritage Site (Listed 1987) Mausoleum of the First Qin Emperor, http://www.whc.unesco.org.

United States Congress (nd) Jonathan O. Moseley (id: M0011023), *Biographical Directory of the United States Congress*. https://en.wikipedia.org/wiki/Biographical_Directory_of_the_United_States_.

United States Department of Health and Human Services, http://www.hhs.gov/aspr/opeo/ndms/teams/dmort.html.

United State Patent and Trademark Office (1848) Patent No. 5,920, Almond D. Fisk, Improvement in Coffins.

Vidette, *Times-Picayune* (1886) Gotham Gossip, 23 August.

Vigorita, V. J. (2008) *Orthopaedic Pathology*. Philadelphia PA: Lippincott Williams & Wilkins.

Walsh, J. P. (2010) Eliphalet Adams Bulkeley, *Connecticut's Heritage Gateway*. http://www.ctheritage.org/encyclopedia/ct1818_1865/bulkeley.htm.

Waugh, A. E. (1968) *Samuel Huntington and His Family*. Stonington CT: Pequot Press.

Weed, H. E. (1912) *Modern Park Cemeteries*. Chicago IL: R. J. Haight.

Winburn, A. P., Schoff, S. K. and Warren, M. W. (2016) Assemblages of the dead: Interpreting the biocultural and taphonomic signature of Afro-Cuban Palo practice in Florida. *Journal of African Disapora Archaeology & Heritage* 5 (1), 1–37.

Woodward, S. L and McDonald, J. N. (2002) *Indian Mounds of the Middle Ohio Valley: A Guide to Mounds and Earthworks of the Adena, Hopewell, Cole, and Fort Ancient People*. Blacksburg VA: McDonald & Woodward Publishing.

Woodward, W. W. (2010) *Prospero's America: John Winthrop Jr., Alchemy and the Creation of New England Culture 1606–1676*. Chapel Hill NC: University of North Carolina Press.

Zimmerman, M. R. and Kelley, M. A. (1982) *Atlas of Human Paleopathology*. New York: Praeger.

Zimmerman, S. J. (1979) The Elisha Pitkin House. *National Register Inventory-Nomination Form*. Hartford CT, Connecticut State Historical Preservation Office.

Index

References in *italics* are pages with illustrations or tables

Aché, 99–101, 105; *See also* Palo Mayombe
Adams
    Abigail, 58
    John, 58
Adena Culture, 27, 111
Adgate, Rebecca, 58
adipocere, 63, 111
Aetna Life Insurance Company, 48
Agra, India, 27
Agricultural Revolution, 26
Albert Morgan Archaeological Society, 81
Allen, Jane, 36
Alsop
    families, 81, 95
    Joseph, 81
    Mary, 79
    mausoleum; *See* Alsop-Chauncey-Mütter Mausoleum
    Richard, 79
Alsop and Company, 81
Alsop-Chauncey-Mütter Mausoleum, *78*, 79–80; *See also* Chauncey Tomb
American Civil War, 92, 95, 105
American Cup Committee, 107
American Revolution, 7, 11, 23–25, 46–47, 59–60, 94; *See also* Revolutionary War
Amiens, France, 81
Amy, 107
Anglican Church, 36, 112
ankylosing spondylitis, 50, 111
archaeological field techniques, 89
Archer, Sarah Elizabeth, 95
Arlington National Cemetery (Virginia), 72
Armed Forces DNA Identification Laboratory, 16
Armed Forces Institute of Pathology, 48
Arthur, Chester A., 92–93, 95
Articles of Confederation, 61
Aspinwall, William, 82–83, *83*; *See also* Panamanian Railroad
Astor, John Jacob, 92

Avery
    Catherine, 94
    Mary, 94
Bacon Academy, 33, 35, 47, 94
Barbian, Lenore, 48
Bastis, Kristen, 42, 48
Bedfordshire, England, 36
Belle Grove, Virginia, 72
Binninger, Miss, 107
Black Rock State Park, 90, 103
Boston (Massachusetts), 36, 58, 80, 93
Boston University, 41
Brick Presbyterian Church, 92, *93*
Bristol
    England, 93
    Rhode Island, 58
Britain, 20, 113–14; *See also* England
    Great, 59
Bulkeley
    Abigail Robbins, 38, 44–46, 52
    Daniel, 45, 47, 49
    Edward, 36
    Eliphalet Adams, 47–48
    Epaphroditus, 45, 47, 50
    genealogy, 43
    Gershom (b.1636), 36–38
    Gershom (tomb builder/patriarch), 38–40, 43–47, 50, 53
    Rev. John, 35, 37–38
    John (brother), 47
    John (son), 42, 45, 47
    Joshua, 45, 49
    Judith Worthington, 45, 52
    Lydia Smith Morgan, 48
    Morgan Gardner, 48, *48*, 92
    Rev. Peter, 36, 38, 43, 80
    Peter (brother), 43, 45–47, 49, 52
    Peter (descendant), 35, 41, 52
    Rhoda Jones Kellogg, 43–45

Roger, 43, 45
Sarah Chauncy, 36–37, 81
Tomb, 14, 33–35, *35*, 39–40, *40*, 41–42, 46, 50, 52, *52*, 55, 57
    coffin materials and artifacts, 40, 43–44, *43–44*, 47, *47*, 50–52, *51*
    desecration and loss of, 33–34
    design, 40
    examination, archaeological and forensic, 35, 39–50, *40–42, 44–47, 49, 51*
    pathological analysis, 48–50
    rediscovery, 34, *35*
    reinternment in, *51*, 52–53
    restoration, 34, 46, *52, 53*
    stone marker, *34, 52*
William (grandson), 45, 49, 52
William (son), 47
Bunker Hill, Battle of, 94
burial vault; *See* vault

Caesar (captive), 39
Cambridge, Massachusetts, 36, 79
Cambridge (university), 36, 80
Cape Horn, 83–84
Carter, Howard, 39
Carver, H. Wayne II, 35, 42, 91; *See also* Office of the State's Chief Medical Examiner
Castro, Fidel, 100
Cedar Hill Cemetery, *12*, 13, 15, 48, 92, 95, 96–98, *96*, 105, 107, 109
cenotaph, 18, 111
Center Cemetery, 14–15, 18–21, *19*, 26, 28–30, 32, 40
Chagres River, 83
Charlemagne, 81
Chauncey
    Rev. Charles (Chauncy), 36, 38, 80–81, *80*
    Charles Alsop, 82, 85–86, 88
    families, 81, 95
    Frederick, 88
    Henry, 14, 75, 77, 81–88, *83*
        career; *See* Panamanian Railroad
        tribute to; *See* SS Henry Chauncey
    Rev. Israel (Chauncy), 81
    Lucy Alsop, 80, 82, 84–89
    mausoleum 95; *See also* Alsop-Chauncey-Mütter Mausoleum
    Nathaniel (fifth), 81
    Rev. Nathaniel, 38, 81
    Richard Alsop, 82, 85
    Sarah (Chauncy); *See* Bulkeley
    Tomb, 14, 75, 77, 78–82, *78*, 85, 95, 97, 101
        coffin materials and artifacts, 81–82, 85–88, *85–88*
        criminal investigation, 75–77, 81–82, 85–89, *85–87*
        design, 81
        examination, archaeological and forensic, 75–77, 81–82, 85–89
Cherokee Nation, 72
Chetwood, Grace, 36
Chexbris, Switzerland, 85
China, 27
Church & Allen Funeral Services, 67, 69
City Beautiful Movement, 11–12, 79
Clarke, Sarah, 58
clay pot (terracotta/ceramic), 90–92, *91*, 99, 101–5, *102–5*
coffin wear, 64, 77
Cogswell
    Rev. James, 55
    Mason Fitch, 55
Colchester (Connecticut), 14, 33–35, 37–39, 41–42, 46–48, 52, 94
    Burial Ground, 14, 33–35, 39, 52
    Historical Society, 41, 52
    Public Works, 35
Colt, Samuel, *12*
Concord (Massachusetts), 23, 36, 38, 59, 115
Confederation Congress, 60
Congregational Church, 3, 9, 22–23, 33, 37, 112
Conlogue, Gerald (Jerry), 91, 97, 101, 108; *See also* Quinnipiac University
Connecticut, 3–4, 6–7, 9–15, 17–19, 22–25, 28, 30, 32–34, 36–38, 41–43, 46–48, 52, 54–55, 58–62, 64, 67, 69, 75–76, 78–79, 81, 90, 92, 94–97, 100, 103, 105
    General Statutes, 7
    Historical Society, 52
    River, 19, 22–23, 25, 37, 79
    State Archaeologist; *See* State Archaeologist
    State Museum of Natural History, 52
    University of, 6, 41–43, 48, 67, 81, 97
Connecticut Colony, 19, 22–23, 32, 59, 79
    General Assembly, 22, 24, 38, 47, 59
    militia, 22–23, 38
Connecticut Gravestone Network, 28, 41
Connecticut Mutual Life Insurance Company, 47
Constellation, *108*
Constitution, Federal, 61
Continental Army, 47
Contois, Jenny, 35
Cooke
    David G. (Dave), 28, 34–35, 39, 41, 67, 69–70, 77, 81
    June, 34
Coolidge, Calvin, 72

Cooperstown, New York, 48
Cornwallis, General Charles, 25
crime scene investigation, 7, 16–17, 81
Cromwell, Connecticut, 75, 77, 82
Crow-Bar Governor, 48; *See also* Bulkeley, Morgan Gardner
crypt; *See* tomb

Dada, 90, 99
Daly, Susan Bulkeley, 41
Day of Resurrection, 8, 20, 113
Declaration of Independence, 54–55, 59–60, *60*
degenerative joint disease, 49
Delta Kappa Epsilon, 105
Department of Defense, 16
Department of Health & Human Services, 16
Devotion, Ebenezer, 55, 59
diffuse idiopathic skeletal hyperostosis (DISH), 49–50, 113
Disaster Mortuary Operational Response Team (DMORT), 16
Disbrow, Mercy Holbridge, 37
Dodd
    Christopher, 69
    Jackie, 69
Dunster, Rev. Henry, 80–81
Durham, Connecticut, 81

East Haddam, Connecticut, 3–4
    Historical Society, 3
East Hartford, Connecticut, 10, 14–15, 18–20, 22–26, 28–30, 32, 35
    Public Works, 28
East Side, 19, 22–25; *See also* East Hartford
Eaton
    Hubert L., 14
    Theophilus, 94
Egypt, 27
Egyptian, 12, 20, 27
England, 22, 26, 36, 58, 80–81, 93, 112
    Church of, 36, 112; *See also* Anglican Church
    Elizabethan, 93
English Parliament, 23, 80
Eyre, Catherine, 81

Fawkes, Guy, 80
First Congregational Church Cemetery, 3, *4*
First Great Awakening, 22–23, 113
Fisk Metallic Burial Case, 20–21, *21*, 25, 28, 31, 113
Fisk, Almond Dunbar, 20, 113

Flora
    (captive, Bulkeley) 39
    (captive, Pitkin) 25
forensic anthropology, 16–17, 89
forensic archaeology, 15–17, 89
Forest Lawn Memorial Park, 14
Fort William Henry, 38
Forty-Niners, 83–84
Franklin, Benjamin, 58
Frémont, John C., 94
French and Indian War, 22, 38, 114
French soldiers, 25, 62
Freneau, Philip, 54
Friends of Center Cemetery, Inc., 20, 28, 32
Friends of the Office of State Archaeology, Inc. (FOSA), 6, 28, 41, 67

Gardner-Bulkeley Cemetery Association, Inc., 35, 52
Garfield, James, 71
Gates/Troop tomb, *4*
George III (king of Great Britain), 23, 59–60
Gilded Age, 12, 107
    "Poster Boy" 105; *See also* Morgan, Edwin D., III
Glamorgan, South Wales, 93
Glendale, California, 14
Gloucester (Massachusetts), 93
Goodwin, Hannah, 21–22
Governor's First Company Foot Guard, 68–69, *68*
Grant's Tomb, 71
Grant, Ulysses S., 71, 92–93
Great Awakenings, 11; *See also* First Great Awakening
Great Puritan Migration, 36, 112
Gregorian calendar, 64–65
Grgurich, Tania, 108
Griswold, Bill, 97
Grove Street Cemetery, 11–12

Harding, Warren, 71–72
Hardy
    Emma, 6
    Thomas, 3, 6, 14, 33–34
Harper
    Albert B. (Al), 28–31, 41–42
    Ross, 51
Harrison, Katherine, 37
Hartford (Connecticut), 12–13, 15, 19, 22, 47–48, 59, 81, 92, 94–97, 100, 105
    County Court 22
Hartford Police Department, 92, 97

Harvard, 36, 38, 80–81, 105–6
    College, 36–37, 80
    Hasty Pudding Club, 105
    President, 36, 38, 80
Hasty Pudding Club, 105
Hawaii, 16
Henry V (king of England), 93
Henry C. Lee Institute of Forensic Sciences, 28, 42
Hepburn
    Katherine, 13
    family tombstone, *13*
Heritage, The, 72
Hertfordshire (England) 80
Hildegard (Charlemagne's queen), 81
Hill, Margery, 94
Hockanum River, 25
Hollywood Cemetery, 72
Hopewell Culture, 27, 114
hora fugit, 10
House of the Night, The (Freneau), 54
Huang, Qin Shi, 27
Hudson River Heights, 25
Huit, Rev. Ephraim, 9
    burial marker, *9*
Hunt, David, 108
Huntington
    Channing M., II, 69
    Frances, 55
    Hannah, 55
    Joseph, 58
    Joseph (brother), 55
    Margaret, 58
    Martha, 14, 54, 57, 59, 61, 68, 70
        skeletal remains, 62–67, *63*
    Mehetable Thurston, 58
    Nathaniel, 58–59
    Samuel, 14, 54–55, *55*, 57–61, 65, 68, 70
        funeral, 54–55
        skeletal remains, 62–66
    Samuel (nephew), 55
    Simon, 58
    Simon, Jr., 58
    Tomb, 14, 54–58, *57*, 62–65, *67*, 67–71, *70*
        coffin material and artifacts, 63–66, *63*, *65–66*
        design, 55, 57
        examination, archaeological and forensic, 57, *57*, 62–67, *67*, 69
        pathological analysis, 31
        reinternment ceremony, 68–70, *68–70*
        restoration, 56–57, *56–57*, 62, 67–68, *67*, 70–72

Indian; *See* Native American
Indian Hill Cemetery, 15, 77–81, 84, 95
Indigenous Peoples; *See* Native American
Industrial Revolution, 12

Jack (captive), 39
Jack (captive, son of Peg), 39
Jackson
    Andrew, 71–72
    Rachel, 72
Jahan, Shah, 27
Jay, John, 60
Jefferson, Thomas, 58
Jones
    Indiana, 82
    Spencer, 44
Joslin, Joseph, Jr., 47
Julian calendar, 64

Kennedy, John F., 72
Killingly, Connecticut, 11
King Arthur, 93
King Philip's War, 19, 37, 114

Lafayette, General (Marquis de), 62
Lake George, 38
Larson, Timothy D., 32
Laud, Rev. William, 80
Lexington (Massachusetts), 23, 47, 94
Lexington, Battle of, 47
Library of Congress, 4
Lincoln
    Abraham, 71, 94–95
    Mary Todd, 71
    Robert Todd, 71
Lishan Mountain, 27
Liverant, Arthur, 34–35
Lord, Mary, 22
Lucumi, 100, 103, 116; *See also* Santeria

Macauda, Mark, 67
Mahal, Mumtaz, 27
Marble Cemetery, 72
Mariel Boatlift, 100
Marion, Ohio, 72
Maryland Archaeological Conservations Laboratories, Inc., 52
Mattabeseck, 79; *See also* Middletown
mausoleum, 6, 20, 27, 33, 71–72, 77–82, 84, 86, 88, 92, 95–97
Mausolus, 27

McKinley, William, 48
McWeeney, Lucinda, 50
Medical Examiner's Office; *See* Office of the State's Chief Medical Examiner
memento mori, 10
Memorial (Lawn) Parks, 14
Metropolitan Museum of Art, 96
Miami, Florida, 100
Middle East, 27
Middletown (Connecticut), 15, 75, 77–79, 81, 84–85, 88–89, 95, 97
Middletown Police Department, 75, 77, 89
Miner Cemetery, 75
Mississippi River Valleys, Ohio and, 27
Mohegan, 22
    Nation, 69
Monroe, James, 71–72
Moretown, Vermont, 43
Morgan
    Alfred Waterman, 95
    Alfred Waterman, Jr.; *See* Morgan, Edwin D., III
    Caroline Matilda, 95
    Edwin D., II, 95, 105
    Edwin D., III, 92, 95, 105–8, *106*
    Edwin Denison, Governor, 15, 48, 92–99, *92*, 102, 105–7, 109
        career, 94–95
        coffin, *98*
        cousin, 48
        funeral, 92–93
        lineage, 92–93
        skeletal remains, 90–91, 97, 99, *99*, 101–2, *102*, 105, 109
        tomb; *See* Tomb
        wife and children, 95
        will, 106–7
    Eliza; *See* Waterman, Eliza Matilda
    Frederick Avery, 95
    Gilbert Henry, 95
    J. Pierpont, 48, 92
    James, 93–94
    Jasper, Deacon, 94
    John, 94
    Mary Brewer Penniman, 91–92, 95, 97–99, *99*, 105–9
        coffin, *98*
        skeletal remains, 90–91, *99*, *108*, 109
    Nathan, 94
    Tomb, 15, 90, 92, 96–97, *96*, *98*, 99, 105, 107, 109
        criminal investigation, 90–92
        design, 96–97
        examination, archaeological and forensic, 91–92, 97–99, 101–5, 108–9

        reinternment in, 109
    Rev. William F., 106
Moroch, Stanley, 35, 41
Mortimer Burying Ground, 79
Moseley
    Jonathan Ogden, 3–6, 11
    Thomas, 3, 6
    Tomb, 3–6
        examination, archaeological and forensic, 3–6
        restoration, 3, 5
Mount Auburn (cemetery), 79
Mount Holly, New Jersey, 84
Mount Vernon (estate), 71
Mullins, Joe, 108
Musketaquid, 36, 115
Mütter
    families, 81, 95
    mausoleum; *See* Alsop-Chauncey-Mütter Mausoleum

Narragansett Bay (Rhode Island), 107
National Baseball Hall of Fame, 48
National Museum of Health and Medicine (Maryland), 48
Native American, 7, 37–38, 78–79, 94, 111, 114
    rebellion, 37; *See also* King Philip's War
    rights, 37–38
Neanderthals, 26
Neolithic period, 26
New Britain (Connecticut), 90, 92, 97, 99–100
New Britain Police Department, 90–91, 97
New England, 6–12, 14, 31, 36–37, 49, 57–58, 62, 79–81, 112, 114
    Christian burials in, 8
    Colonies, 20
    genealogists, 22
    headstone, *10*
    indigenous in habitants of; *See* Native American
    minister, 81
    tombs and vaults, 6–7, 11, 20, 57
New England Witch Trials, 37
New Haven (Connecticut), 11–12, 94
    University of, 28, 41–42
New London, Connecticut, 36–37, 94
New York City, 16, 71–72, 81, 84, 88, 92–96, 105–7
New York Times, 95, 106–7
New York Yacht Club, 107
New-Light; *See* First Great Awakening
Newport, Rhode Island, 25, 105, 107
Nile River, 27

Norwich (Connecticut), 14, 54–59, 61–62, 67–70
    Historical Society, 57, 68
Norwichtown (Connecticut), 14, 54, 56, 62
    Burying Ground, 14, 54–57, 67–70

Oak Ridge Cemetery, 71
Obliterate Tomb, The (Hardy), 3, 6, 14, 33
occult, 7, 17, 37, 77–78, 88–89, 101; *See also* Palo Mayombe; Santeria
Odell (England), 36
Office of State Archaeology, 7, 57
Office of the State's Chief Medical Examiner, 7, 42, 91–92, 97, 101
Ohio
    and Mississippi River Valleys, 114
    Historical Society, 72
    Marion, 72
Olcott, Abigail, 81
Old-Lights; *See* First Great Awakening
Oregon/California Trail, 83
Orisha, 99–100; *See also* Santeria
osteomyelitis, 49, 66, 115
osteoporosis, 31, 49, 115

Palisado Cemetery, 9, *9–10*
Palo Mayombe (Palo), 78, 90–91, 100–101, 105
Panama, 84
    Canal, 82
    City, 83
    Colon, 81
Panamanian Railroad, 81–85
Peg (captive), 39
Penniman
    George Henry, 106
    Margaret, 106
    Mary Brewer; *See* Morgan
periodontal disease, 31, 50, 115
Philadelphia (Pennsylvania), 47, 59
Pitkin
    A.P., 18, 28
    Clarissa Roberts, 21, 28, 31
    Clarissa, Jr., 28, 30–31
    Edward, 20–21, 25, 28–29, 31
        coffin; *See* Fisk Metallic Burial Case
    Electa Kimball, 32
    Elisha (2), 31–32
    Elisha, Squire, 14, 18, 22–26, *23*, 29, 31–32
        house, 24–25, *24*
    Elizabeth, 32
    family reunion, 32
    Fort, 19
    genealogy, 18, 28–29, 31
    Hannah, 32
    Hannah (wife), 31–32
    Horace, 31–32
    James, Capt., 22
    Jerusha, 31
    Joseph, 22
    Mary Cheney, 32
    Roswell, 32
    Roswell, Jr., 31
    Samuel, 32
    Samuel L., 32
    Sarah 32,
    Sarah Ann, 32
    Solomon, 31–32
    Stephen, 31–32
    Timothy, 31
    Tomb, 14, 18, 19–20, *19*, *21*, 26, 28–29, *29*, 32
        design, 18–19, 28
        examination, archaeological and forensic, 20, *21*, 28–32, *29–30*
        memorial stone, *32*
        pathological analysis, 31
        restoration, 20
        signage, 14–15, *15*
    William (2), 22
    William (3), Governor, 22–23, 26
    William the Immigrant, 20, 22
Pittsburgh, Pennsylvania, 94
Plum, Samuel, 75
Plymouth (Massachusetts), 80–81, 112
pot (vessel); *See* clay pot
Prentice, Sarah, 37
priest (ritual), 90, 99–100; *See also* Dada
Prince (captive), 39
Puritan, 8–10, 23, 36–38, 58, 80, 112
Putnam, Israel, 47, 94

Quick Response (QR) Code, 14–15
Quinnipiac University, 91, 97, 101, 108
    Bioanthropology Research Institute, 101, 108
    Department of Diagnostic Imaging, 101

Republican Party, 94
Revolutionary War, 19, 24; *See also* American Revolution; War of Independence
Rise of Civilization, 27
rituals; *See* occult; *Palo Mayombe*; Santeria
Robbins, Abigail; *See* Bulkeley
Rochambeau, General Comte de, 24–25, *25*
Rocky Hill, Connecticut, 14, 28
Rogers, Anna Bulkeley, 45, 52
Rohon, David, 90–91
Rose Hill Cemetery, 14
Roure, Cara, 67

Rowland, John G., 69
Roxbury (Massachusetts), 58, 94
rural cemetery movement, 11–12, 79

Saginaw, Michigan, 4
Saint-Gaudens, Augustus, 96
San Francisco (California), 83–84
Santeria, 17, 78, 90, 100–101, 116
Saybrook, Connecticut, 81
Scituate, Massachusetts, 80
Scotland (Connecticut), 55, 58
Second Continental Congress, 54, 59–61
Seven Wonders of the Ancient World, 27
Shaanxi Province, 27
Shakespeare, William, 8
Silver Lane, 25
Simmons, Rob, 69
Sledzik, Paul, 48
Smithsonian Institution, 108
Sonntag, Mary Catherine, 91–92, 107
Sons of Liberty, 59
Sons of the American Revolution, 68
Sowheag (sachem), 79
Spaulding, John J., 28, 30, 32, 35, 41, 43, 67
Springfield, Illinois, 71
SS *Henry Chauncey*, *84*, 84
SS *Oregon*, 106–7
St John's College, Cambridge, 36
Stamp Act 1765, 23, 59
Stanley
　Elizabeth, 22
　William (Bill), 68
State Archaeologist, 3, 6–7, 15, 19, 57, 75, 78, 81, 92, 97
Stephens, John Lloyd, 82, *83*, 83–84
Stevens, Paran, 107
Stone, Horatio, 79
Stoughton, Thomas, 58
Suessman, Doris, 20

Taintor, Charles, 42, 45
Taj Mahal, 27
Tanner (captive), 25
Thompson, Roger, 35
tomb, 6–8, 11–12, 14–15, 17, 26–27
　restoration, 3, 5–6, 15, 20, 34, 46, 56–57, 62, 67–68, 70–72
　vandalism, 3, 6–7, 11, 15, 28, 30, 40, 57–58, 65, 71–72, 77–78, 81–82, 85–89, 92, 97, 99, 101, 109
　See also Bulkeley; Chauncey; Morgan; Mosely; Pitkin
Townshend Act, 23

Trail of Tears, 72
Trinity College, Cambridge, 80
Trumbull
　John, 46
　Jonathan, 46, 49
　Joseph, 46
Tutankhamen, 39
Tyler, John, 72
typhoid, 105, 107

Ullinger, Jaime, 97
Uncas (sachem), 22
United Kingdom, 32; *See also* Britain; England

Valparaiso, Chile, 81
Van Dyke, Rev. Henry J., Jr., 95
Vanderbilt, Cornelius, 96
vault, 6, 11; *See also* tomb
Victorian era, 12

Wachuset Hill (Massachusetts), 37
Wangunk Tribe, 78–79
War of Independence, 62; *See also* American Revolution; Revolutionary War
Ward, Relford "Mitch", 75
Ware (England), 80
Washington
　George, 25, 47, 58, 61, 65, 71
　Martha, 71
Washington (Massachusetts), 94
Waterman, Eliza Matilda, 92, 95, 106
Watertown, Connecticut, 90
Welles, Sarah Bulkeley Trumbull, 45–46, 50
Wesleyan University, 41
West Indies Trade, 24, 46
Westminster, 80
Wethersfield (Connecticut), 37
White, Stanford, 96
William the Conqueror, 81
Williams, Elizabeth, 94
Windham (Connecticut), 58–59, 65
Windsor (Connecticut), 9, 58, 94
Winthrop, John Jr., 37
World Trade Center, 16

Yale College, 23, 47, 81
Yarmouth, England, 58
Yorick (*Hamlet*), 8
Yorktown (Virginia), 25
Yoruba, 100, 103, 116
Yznaga
　Fernando, 107
　Jennie, 107